DECLARATION
ON
RELIGIOUS FREEDOM
OF
VATICAN COUNCIL II

DECLARATION
ON
RELIGIOUS FREEDOM
OF
VATICAN COUNCIL II

Promulgated by Pope Paul VI
December 7, 1965

Commentary by
THOMAS F. STRANSKY, C.S.P.

1966
VATICAN II DOCUMENTS
PAULIST PRESS
NEW YORK   GLEN ROCK   WESTMINSTER
TORONTO   AMSTERDAM

Nihil Obstat:
Rev. James J. O'Connor
Censor Librorum

Imprimatur:
✠ Leo A. Pursley, D.D.
Bishop of Fort Wayne-South Bend
November 28, 1966

The Nihil Obstat and Imprimatur are official declarations that
a book or pamphlet is free of doctrinal or moral error. No
implication is contained therein that those who have granted
the Nihil Obstat and Imprimatur agree with the contents,
opinions, or statements expressed.

Cover Design: Claude Ponsot

Published by Paulist Press
Editorial Office: 304 W. 58th St., N.Y., N.Y. 10019
Business Office: Glen Rock, New Jersey 07452

Printed in the
United States of America
by Our Sunday Visitor Press

Contents

Contents

Commentary

HISTORY AND DEVELOPMENT
OF
THE DECLARATION
1960–1965

PREPARATORY PHASE
1960–1962

On November 14-15, 1960, six months after Pope John had created the Secretariat for Promoting Christian Unity, its members and consultors—bishops and priests but, regretfully, no laity—assembled in Rome for its first meeting. They had to spell out the implications of that simple but vague marching order of the pope: the Secretariat would enable "those who bear the name of Christians but are separated from this Apostolic See . . . to follow the work of the [Second Vatican] Council and to find more easily the path by which they may arrive at that unity" for which Christ prayed.[1] The

---

[1] *Superno Dei nutu: A.A.S.* 52 (1960), p. 436. This personal executive order *(motu proprio)* of Pope John set up ten commissions and three secretariats to begin the immediate preparations for the Council.

group drew up a list of topics that directly or indirectly would influence the ecumenical dimension of the Council. Fourth on the list was *De libertate religiosa*.[2] A corresponding subcommission was formed.[3]

From its very beginnings, the Secretariat had an internal consensus that would never weaken. This conviction would be expressed by the Secretariat spokesman, Bishop Emile de Smedt, when he first introduced the religious freedom theme to the Council fathers on November 19, 1963: "Many non-Catholics harbor an aversion against the Church, or at least suspect it of a kind of Machiavellianism, because we seem to them to demand free exercise of religion when Catholics are in a minority in any nation and at the same time refuse and deny the same religious freedom when Catholics are in a majority."[4]

Why speak about dialogue with other Chris-

---

[2] In the autumn of 1960 Pope John gave the preparatory groups a small brochure of suggested themes for their work. There is no mention either of religious freedom or of tolerance. In April, 1961, the commissions received for their confidential use twelve volumes of "suggestions and wishes" (*consilia et vota*) which had been submitted by all the world's archbishops and bishops, major superiors of male religious orders, theological faculties of Catholic universities and other institutes of learning, and the Roman curial organs. In the two-volume index (which excludes the reports from the curia and the universities), of the 8,972 catalogued items, only eight concern "tolerance": "What is to be thought of that freedom, not only religious but also civil and political, which pertains to both Catholics and non-Catholics?"

[3] The original members: Bishops Francois Charrière of Switzerland (chairman) and Emile Josef de Smedt (Belgium); Fathers Gregory Baum, O.S.A. (Canada), Jerome Hamer, O.P. (France) and Gustave Weigel, S.J. (U.S.A.).

[4] The entire speech is found below as Appendix I, pp. 93-108.

tians, with Jews, with all non-Christians, if, in theory or in fact, the Roman Catholic Church does not respect the freedom of non-Catholics? Religious freedom is a precondition for any genuine trust in ecumenical life—in fact, in relations with anyone, whether Christian or non-Christian. Other Christians were especially sensitive to the conciliar issue. "Every ecumenical 'move' of the Catholic Church will be completely fruitless and devoid of any real meaning unless the Church states clearly and authoritatively that it will respect the liberty of other believers, even if it has the power or the occasion to do otherwise, and that it condemns intolerance, persecution and discrimination on grounds of religious liberty." [5]

The Secretariat, however, wanted the Council to do more than sanction a "policy change" based on mere social or political expediency or on correct ecumenical tactics. It would plead for a deepening and development of the doctrine of religious freedom. Bishop de Smedt would tell the Council fathers: "The Church must teach and defend the right to religious freedom because there is a question of the truth, care of which was committed to it by Christ." [6] At the same time, the

---

[5] Dr. A. F. Carrillo de Albornoz, the Secretary for Religious Liberty in the World Council of Churches, "Religious Liberty and the Second Vatican Council," in *The Ecumenical Review* (July, 1964), p. 395. An informal and unpublicized consultation on religious freedom was held in May, 1961, between Roman Catholic and W.C.C. experts. Monsignor Jan Willebrands, Secretary of the Vatican Unity Secretariat, and Father Hamer participated. The World Council of Churches had already published a *Declaration on Religious Liberty* at its First Assembly in Amsterdam (1948), and was soon to issue a *Statement on Religious Liberty* at its Third Assembly in New Delhi (Dec. 1961). Cf. below, Appendix IV.

[6] Cf. below, p. 93. In fact, in his list of four reasons for

Council should define or describe the full sense and meaning of religious freedom in such a way as to reach at least general agreement among all Christians, indeed among all men of goodwill.[7]

Despite the strong, clear motivation of the Secretariat, the conciliar theme of religious freedom was not graced with easy development. It quickly became burdened with an almost freakish history, and only when the complete records have been published will the heat of the crucible from which the final Declaration emerged be measured with exactness.

From the start of the open debate, an articulate minority would offer little development in its own thinking on the theme, but to the very end this group would be tenacious in its loyal opposition. Yet, despite this advantage of persistent, radical objections in the process of drafting any conciliar document, what would be more fruitful would arise from the difference of opinion among the bishops and theologians who were in favor of religious freedom and who sought the most effective way of presenting the Catholic position through a Council of the Church.

Should the conciliar document present a Christian theology of freedom in the context of which

the conciliar statement, Bishop de Smedt placed the ecumenical reason as fourth, the concern for truth as first.

[7] The United Nations has listed religious liberty provisions in its 1948 *Universal Declaration of Human Rights*. At present the U.N.'s Human Rights Commission is drafting an international treaty to implement these provisions, and in their deliberations the religious freedom declarations of the World Council of Churches and Vatican Council II "are being quoted on the side of freedom". Cf. Dean M. Kelly and Claud D. Nelson, "Religious Liberty: Toward Consensus", in *The Christian Century* (May 18, 1966), p. 651; "Religious Freedom and the U.N.," in *Herder Correspondence* (June, 1964), pp. 163–164.

religious freedom is to be treated? Or should the statement be confined to the issue of the right to freedom in religious matters in the constitutional ordering of society (a *civil* right)? And what arguments should be used to support the thesis? Should they be taken primarily from reason or from the revealed Word of God? How much emphasis should be placed on, and what weight given to, the statements of recent popes? Finally, the answers to the above would depend on the decision taken to the same problem that confronted the drafters of *The Church in the Modern World:* To what audience is the theme addressed? Primarily to Roman Catholics? To Christians in general? Or to all men?

In general, as a result of its conciliar dialogue with both friends and opponents of the successive drafts, the Secretariat itself developed its own thinking on the theme and mode of presentation. Despite the basic divergences among the supporters of the document, the Secretariat found that its continual and laborious work of revision over four sessions so developed, strengthened and clarified a basic orientation and argument in each new draft, that gradually a strong consensus was shaped among the vast majority of the Council fathers.

By August, 1961, the Secretariat had given general approval to its draft, *De Libertate Religiosa* (On Religious Freedom). It had an introduction and three chapters.

The introduction pledges the Church to defend the honor of God and the dignity of the human person created and redeemed by him. In Chapter I, the Church vindicates the right of every man and the religious community, and thus also of those who "err concerning the faith", to religious freedom or immunity from any external coercion. The Church also reprobates discrimination, injuries, or persecutions of men or nations solely because of origins, color or blood.[8] In Chapter II, the Church urges the cooperation of Roman Catholics with all men of goodwill, "whether believers or professing no religion", in the ordering of society "according to the moral norms which flow from the very dignity of the human person". Chapter III was bold in its explanations of "The Relations between the Church and Civil Society". The Church wholly approves of those civil societies which, in the practical ordering of civil life, legally acknowledge religious freedom and political equality for citizens of any religion. The State cannot impose on its citizens the profession of any one religion as a condition for a full, integral participation in national or civic life.

This document was submitted to the Preparatory Central Commission, a large body of 102 members—60 cardinals, 5 patriarchs, 33 archbishops and 4 superior generals of male religious communities. From November, 1961, to June, 1962, this Commission had had to wade through 140 different schemata drawn up by the thirteen preparatory commissions.

The religious freedom document reached the table of the Central Commission at its last meeting, June 18, 1962. But that same day and on that same table rested another document. The Theological Commission had prepared "The Relations between Church and State, and Religious Tolerance". It

---

[8] The general theme of discrimination was eventually dropped from the religious freedom schema, and introduced as the fifth paragraph of the *Declaration on the Relation of the Church to Non-Christian Religions*. Also cf. *Pastoral Constitution on the Church in the Modern World*. n. 29.

was Chapter IX of the bulky document *On the Church (De Ecclesia)*.[9]

There was no surprise at the overlapping of themes and thus at the lack or coordination between the Theological Commission and the Secretariat for Promoting Christian Unity. In the Central Commission's previous discussions on documents from other commissions, it had become annoyingly clear that the Theological Commission had refused collaboration with any other commission that had asked for it. It seemed that the Theological Commission was working on the principle of non-collaboration because it regarded itself as "supreme" in stature. Theology "rules over". Other commissions should restrict their documents only to "practical, pragmatic issues". The Theological Commission alone would prepare for conciliar "theological issues". It would remain aloof from any other commission's attempt to do the same.

What did surprise the Central Commission was the contrast—indeed, the contradictions—between the two documents, especially in their treatment of the proper mission and competency of civic authority.

As an extreme example, the Secretariat draft concluded its argument: "The State should be impartial, loyal and fair toward all who obey the dictates of conscience in religious matters." But the

---

9 The chapter, in only seven pages of text but with fifteen pages of footnotes, had six paragraphs: (1) the distinction between the Church and civil authority, and the subordination of the end of the State to the end of the Church; (2) the power of the Church and its limits, and the duties of the Church toward civil powers; (3) the general principle of applying these principles; (4) application in a Catholic State; (5) religious tolerance in a non-Catholic State; (6) conclusion.

De Ecclesia schema concluded: The ideal State is the "Catholic State", and in such a State "the civic power should protect its citizens from seducing errors and thus preserve the unity of faith—the highest good. . . ." The civic power "can temper public manifestations of other (i.e., non-Roman Catholic) cults and defend its citizens against the diffusion of false doctrines which, in the Church's judgment, place external salvation in danger".

What would become clearer in the conciliar process over the next four years would be the presuppositions for such divergent conclusions.[10]

Should both documents be placed before the Council fathers? In July, 1962, three months before the first session opened, Pope John created a small commission to discuss the issue. It was composed of the two Presidents and the two Secretaries of the Theological Commission (Cardinal Ottaviani and Father Tromp), and the Secretariat for Christian Unity (Cardinal Bea and Monsignor Willebrands). The fifth member was a "neutral", Cardinal Ciriaci. But this special commission never met!

---

[10] The official *L'Osservatore Romano* account of the June 18th meeting did not allude to any conflict. Furthermore, the report gave the impression that both drafts concern exclusively the rights of the Roman Catholic Church, independent of any civil power, to preach the Gospel and to offer true worship. Immediate negative press reaction to this apparent one-sidedness called for a clarification a few days later in the *L'Osservatore Romano* summary of the Central Commission's work. The Secretariat draft treats "especially the right of man to follow the exigencies of his own well-informed conscience, even in religious matters. . . . The State has the duty in practice of respecting this right in its citizenry. . . . a burning issue for our modern pluralistic society, and also extremely difficult". Cf. *Preparatory Reports: Second Vatican Council,* tr. Aram Berard, S.J. (Philadelphia: Westminster, 1965), pp. 200–201; 210.

FIRST SESSION
1962

During the first session, the Secretariat document was neither printed nor distributed to the Council fathers. But in the general discussion on *De Ecclesia,* they did have a chance to comment briefly on its Chapter IX, now entitled, "Relations between Church and State".

This chapter had been somewhat changed from its earlier form. Eliminated were the different applications of a general principle to States where Catholics predominated and to those where Catholics unfortunately were in a minority. Thus, the precise problem of the "religious freedom of Catholics but tolerance of others" was dropped.

The general discussion on the Church, however, did not concentrate on any specific chapter, although Cardinal Joseph Ritter (St. Louis) did insist that the schema should contain a clear statement on liberty of conscience, and Cardinal Franziskus Koenig (Vienna) also noted the absence of this theme. Instead, the fathers severely criticized the whole schema's general approach to the Church's understanding of itself in the modern world—an approach that, in the words of Bishop de Smedt, was triumphalistic, over-clerical and predominantly juridical. A complete redrafting was called for, in which the mystery of the Church as servant predominates, and there is emphasized "a triple dialogue: with the faithful, with our separated brethren and with the world outside the Church" (Cardinal Leo Josef Suenens).

Four months after the first session, Pope John

issued "to all men of goodwill" his own Declaration on "establishing universal peace in truth, justice, charity and freedom", in the form of an encyclical letter, *Pacem in terris* (April, 1963). Its two basic themes—the dignity of the human person and the consequent necessity of constitutional limits to the powers of government—would be the main support of the religious freedom document. One sentence stood out boldly: "Every human being has the right to honor God according to the dictates of an upright conscience (*ad rectam conscientiae suae normam*), and therefore the right to worship God privately and publicly."[11] The encyclical was the last helping terrestrial hand which Pope John offered to the Secretariat's drafting.

The experience of the first session proved that too much material had been prepared. The newly elected Pope Paul created a Coordination Commission that whittled down the forest of drafts to a manageable seventeen. A vote of the first session assured that a new draft on ecumenism would have

---

11 *Pacem in terris*, n. 14 (Glen Rock, N.J.: Paulist Press, 1963), p. 9. In theological tradition *conscientia recta* has two different meanings. For Thomas Aquinas, *recta* means conformity to truth, i.e., to *objective* moral norms. Conscientia *recta* and conscientia *vera* are the same. On the other hand, following Dun Scotus and Suarez, conscientia *recta* means sincere or upright, i.e., formed to the best of one's ability, without bad will. Conscientia recta is either *vera* (in fact conformed to objective truth), or *erronea* (in fact not so conformed, whether intentionally or not). In *Pacem in terris*, which of the two meanings did Pope John intend by "ad rectam conscientiae suae normam"? After the publication of the encyclical, some theologians (e.g., G. de Broglie, S.J.) claimed the first meaning (conscientia recta = vera). Others (e.g., Cardinal Bea and Bishop de Smedt) claimed the second. In 1965, Pietro Pavan, one of Pope John's principal helpers in the drafting, stated that the pope deliberately chose *recta* in order *not* to resolve the theological problem! Cf. Pietro Pavan, *Libertà religiosa e pubblici poteri* (Milan, 1965), p. 357.

future conciliar debate.[12] Accordingly, the Secretariat for Christian Unity maneuvered to attach both its separate drafts on the Jews [13] and on religious freedom as Chapters IV and V of the new ecumenism decree in order that all three subjects would eventually be debated. The Secretariat, on the whole, was in favor of detaching the last two chapters and of treating them as separate documents *after* the assurance of an initial vote of approval of the entire five chapters of *De Oecumenismo* as a sufficient basis for future elaboration. This tactic only half succeeded in the second session.

It should be noted that no United States bishop was a member of the Secretariat during the conciliar preparations and the first session. The American hierarchy was justifiably concerned over this irritating lacuna, since the Secretariat drafts on ecumenism, on the Jews and on religious freedom certainly had prime relevance for the pluralistic situation in the United States.

The Secretariat itself was aware of the lacuna, but could do nothing. Other preparatory commissions had ceased to exist at the opening of the first session, and new ones were formed by conciliar election and papal appointment. But Pope John had made an exception for the Secretariat's structure: it would remain during the Council as it had been during the preparations. In fact, this frozen structure gave the Secretariat only sixteen members who were Council fathers.

Pope Paul, also sensitive to the lack of U.S.

---

12 Cf. *The Decree on Ecumenism,* with a commentary by Thomas F. Stransky, C.S.P. (Glen Rock, N.J.: Paulist Press, 1965) , pp. 9–10.

13 Cf. *The Declaration on the Relation of the Church to Non-Christian Religions,* with a commentary by René Laurentin and Joseph Neuner, S.J. (Glen Rock, N.J.: Paulist Press, 1966) , p. 20.

episcopal representation, appointed to the Secretariat Archbishops John Deardon (Detroit) and Lawrence Shehan (Baltimore) in September, 1963. Both Americans were already members of other conciliar commissions.

Then, toward the end of the second session, Pope Paul decided to increase the membership in all the conciliar commissions up to thirty fathers. Of the twelve needed in the Secretariat, eight were elected by the Council. Two of these were Americans: Bishops Charles Helmsing (Kansas City-St. Joseph) and Ernest Primeau (Manchester). A legal technicality (no father can serve on more than one commission) forced Archbishops Deardon and Shehan to state their preference. The former chose to remain on the important Theological Commission; the latter asked to leave the Seminary Commission for the Secretariat.[14]

---

[14] In a fascinating reversal of roles, the U.S. bishops at Vatican Council I lobbied strongly—and effectively—to keep the religious liberty and Church-State question from reaching the floor. In the middle of the 19th century, and with overwhelming European representation at the Council, the subject certainly was not mature. Cf. James J. Hennesey, *The First Council of the Vatican: The American Experience* (New York: Herder and Herder, 1963).

SECOND SESSION
1963

De Ecclesia returned to the Council floor at the second session, but the new, better composed Theological Commission had revised the draft so drastically that all one could recognize in the new one was the title. The Church-State and religious tolerance issues had been dropped from the new schema. The Unity Secretariat now had firm possession of the theme.

Bishop de Smedt introduced the fifth chapter of *De Oecumenismo* to the Council on November 19, 1963.[15] The chapter, called "On Religious Freedom", was short, only seven pages of text in seven paragraphs.

The Text

The chapter takes a specifically Christian approach to the issue. It is addressed mainly to Catholics. The general theme specifies the respect one should have "not only for the sacred and absolute rights of God and for the truths and objects which should always be honored, but also for the rights and duties of the persons or subjects who are to adhere to the truth" (Introduction).

This theme is divided into two main theses, and the two would remain throughout the document's evolution in the Council:

1. *Every man, by right of nature (jure na-*

---

15 Cf. below, Appendix I, pp. 93-108.

turae), has the right to the free exercise of religion in society according to the dictates of his personal conscience.

The Church is to preach the Good News to all people (cf. Mt. 28, 19-20). It exhorts its faithful to walk in wisdom as regards those not in their company (cf. Col. 4, 5). They should "diffuse the light of life by those means of nature and grace which the Lord himself has used: that is, by the preaching of doctrine, by living example, and by bearing witness to the truth, even to the shedding of one's own blood" (n. 1).

At the same time, the Christian faithful are to recognize "the progressive and human way by which God draws men to his truth and love. Therefore, one must respect not only the duties toward the life-giving Word which must be preached, but also to the rights and the measuring out of grace which belong to the person, invited by God to be drawn freely to the faith". The Word of God is spoken freely to man; it is for man to respond to it freely or not at all. No man may abdicate the responsibility to respond; no man can assume responsibility for another (n. 2).

"Since the human person, gifted with conscience and free activity, can fulfill the will of God only insofar as he perceives the divine law through the dictates of conscience, he can reach his final end only by prudently forming the judgments of conscience and by faithfully carrying out its dictates. Therefore, the one who sincerely obeys his conscience intends to obey God himself, even though sometimes confusedly and unknowingly." As long as man is "in invincible error, he is worthy of respect, and his religious freedom is acknowledged and vindicated by the Church" (n. 3).

In short, "religious freedom, or immunity from external coercion is postulated by the nature of the act of faith" (n. 2) and by the nature of man's conscience (n. 3). This is not religious indifferentism. One does not affirm that truth and error are equal in the sight of God. One must, however, affirm the dignity of the human person and the freedom of the act of personal religious decision, whether this is that of an individual or of groups of men (n. 4).

2. *The juridical consequences of the right to religious freedom obliges other men in society, especially the State, to acknowledge this personal right, to respect it in practice and to promote its free exercise.*

The external, public exercise of freedom of conscience "cannot be impeded unless it contradicts the common good or the objective order of both the rights of God and the unalienable rights and liberties of the human person".

"The Council solemnly declares that the attempts to wipe out religion itself, either in the whole human race or in a specific religious group, most clearly and most gravely injures the rights of the creator and savior of men and the most sacred rights of the human conscience and the family of nations.

"The public powers cannot impose on citizens the profession of any one religion as a condition for the full and integral right to take part in civic and national life. Human powers should observe justice and equity toward all those who obey the dictates of their conscience in matters religious.

"Likewise, religious freedom is offended against, above all, by the death sentence for religious reasons, and also when, on account of one's religion, his possessions are confiscated, or he is deprived of the things required for decent living, or is denied social and civic equality or citizenship, competency for civil processes and the exercise of those fundamental rights which nations recognize by common consent" (n. 5).

The Secretariat draft concludes with a plea that all who bear the name of Christ—indeed, that all men of goodwill, whether they profess religious faith or not—"cooperate in the ordering of society according to the moral norms which flow from the very dignity of the human person" (n. 6). And for the Christian, there is a higher norm—charity. "The task of perfecting creation and the service to society, intrinsic to every activity which affects the goods of human culture, are ordained by charity to the building up of the Church (cf. 1 Cor. 24, 5) and to the glory of God (cf. 1 Cor. 10, 31)" (n. 7).

Far longer, and perhaps more convincing than the text itself, was the brilliantly rhetorical introductory speech by Bishop de Smedt. He asked the fathers not to give to the term "religious freedom" a meaning that differs from the one intended by the text. The expression does *not* mean that: (1) it is proper for a man to consider the religious problem according to his own whim without any moral obligation and decide for himself according to his own will whether or not to embrace religion (religious indifferentism); (2) the human conscience is free in the sense that it is, as it were, outside of the law, absolved from any obligation toward God (laicism); (3) falsehood is to be considered on an equal footing with truth, as though there were no objective order of truth (doctrinal relativism); (4) man has a quasi right to maintain a peaceful complacency in the midst of uncertainty (dilettantistic pessimism).

No, continued the bishop, the document gives another and very precise meaning to the term. "Positively, religious freedom is the right of the human person to the free exercise of religion according to the dictates of his conscience. Negatively, it is immunity from all external force in his personal relations with God, which the conscience of man vindicates to itself."

The Belgian bishop took most of his time in outlining the development of papal teaching, from Pius IX to John XXIII (especially the latter's encyclical, *Pacem in terris*), concerning the duties of public authority in matters religious. He begged the fathers to understand the *development* of the Church's teaching, and not to force the present draft "to speak outside of its historical and doctrinal content—not, in other words, to make the fish swim out of water". But the bishops of the opposition soon would zero in precisely on this Secretariat's claim of legitimate development; its document, they would assert, was a monster fish that could never live within the waters of the Church's teaching.

Bishop de Smedt concluded his speech with what turned out to be a naive promise: the Secretariat, by working "day and night" in studying the fathers' comments, could polish up the document for final conciliar approval at the end of the second session, three weeks away, December 4.

During the general discussion on the *Decree on Ecumenism* (Nov. 19-22), some bishops did comment specifically on its fifth chapter, *De libertate religiosa*, even though they had had little time to study the contents (its distribution was on November 19). There was a question as to the exact placement of the religious freedom topic. Cardinal Bacci wanted a separate document, whereas Bishop Sergio Mendez Arceo (Cuernavaca, Mexico) wanted the theme advanced as Chapter I of *De Oecumenismo* ("It is not an appendix or corollary, but the fundamental principle and perspective. Unity without liberty is not religious"!); Bishop José Pont y Gol (Segorbe-Castellon, Spain), in the name of 70 bishops, agreed. Bishop Ermenegilde Florit (Florence) asked that the topic be transferred to the proposed draft on the Church in the modern world. The Swiss bishops pleaded for more explicit treatment of the freedom of believing *communities*.[16] The bishop for the Argentine Ukrainians asked for a clear and strong condemnation of persecution under militant atheism.

Immediately after the general discussion on all five chapters of *De Oecumenismo* (Nov. 19-21), the Secretary General of the Council, Archbishop Pericles Felici, announced a division of the important initial vote: an immediate vote on the first three chapters; a later vote on the last two. The "later", it turned out, was not during the second session; it would be at the third session for the Jewish theme, the fourth for the religious freedom schema.

The postponement of the vote on Chapters IV and V of the ecumenism schema irritated the vast majority of the Council fathers, despite Cardinal Bea's promise to them on December 2: "What is put off is not put away."

In general, during the second session one witnessed what appeared to be a naive and over-

---

16 In the Swiss Constitution there are still discriminatory laws against Catholics, especially against religious orders (Art. 52 forbids the restoration or creation of new ones; Jesuits are forbidden by Art. 51 to be in charge of churches or schools). Priests cannot be voted in for Congress (Art. 75). The government determines the erection of new dioceses or changes in existing ones (Art. 50).

bouyant optimism among the majority who cockily expected the session to be a simple mopping-up exercise. These fathers tended to forget that a Council succeeds through dialogue, not by voting down the opposition or demanding constant papal interventions. (As Bishop Helder Câmara urged: "Strive to convince, not to conquer.") At the same time the bishops of the majority underestimated the tenacity and resources of those who formed the hard core of resistance to any radical development of Church teaching or practice, and the delay of the vote on religious freedom only helped to harden the minority forces who were determined to delay any kind of vote on religious freedom until after a radical revision of the text could be forced.[17]

The Unity Secretariat still managed to keep control of the revision work.[18] By March, 1964, 380 lengthy observations (280 single-spaced pages) were sent to the drafters by individual bishops or by groups of them. Opinions where to place the docu-

---

[17] Nevertheless, the postponement of the vote meant at least that the first three chapters on ecumenism could be evaluated more calmly, without being prejudiced for different reasons by the far more delicate questions of religious freedom and the Jews, even though these two topics are very related to ecumenism.

[18] After the second session the special Mixed Commission for the "Church in the modern world" draft began its work. Some within the Commission at first thought that at least the substance of the religious freedom schema could be incorporated into this new document in the section on international affairs. But as the whole modern world draft took shape, the Mixed Commission decided against pressing for the incorporation. It judged, as did the Secretariat, that too much of the original schema would be lost in the condensation, and that most likely the debate over the religious freedom theses would intensify. The Mixed Commission was composed of members from the Theological Commission and the Commission on the Lay Apostolate.

ment were obviously conflicting. But more serious were the equally conflicting opinions on the correct approach to the whole theme.

The Coordinating Commission accepted the new draft on April 18, 1964.[19] It decided that this text of the Secretariat and its other one on the world religions should now be submitted to the Council as two Declarations, distinct from, but annexed to, the schema on ecumenism. The fathers had the new document in their hands during the summer of 1964.

---

[19] On the previous day, April 17, Pope Paul addressed the United Nations seminar on freedom of information: "[The problem of religious freedom] is of such importance and scope that the Ecumenical Council took it up. There is every reason to expect the promulgation of a text which will have great consequences not only for the Church but for all those—and they are countless—who will feel themselves affected by an authoritative statement on the subject" (*L'Osservatore Romano,* April 18, 1964) .

THIRD SESSION
1964

At the third session, Bishop de Smedt once more introduced the theme to the fathers on September 23, 1964. The new draft was entitled *Declaratio Prior: de libertate religiosa* to distinguish it from *the Declaratio Altera: de Iudaeis et de Non Christianis*. The general approach had remained the same. The draft addressed itself primarily to Catholics.

The Text

As stated in its official printed report *(relatio)*, the Secretariat had accepted five principal criteria for its revision of the 1963 text.

1. *The meaning and basis of religious freedom should be more clearly expressed.*

There is a distinction between freedom in one's relations with God and freedom in relation with men. The Declaration is concerned exclusively with religious freedom in relation with other men. To make this clear, the Declaration is subtitled, "The right of the individual and communities to freedom in religious matters", and at the very beginning of the new text this strict meaning is stated in both a positive and negative way.

Positively: "Men fashioned in the image of God and called to share in the divine nature have the duty and the honor to follow, according to the

31

dictates of their conscience, the will of their creator and savior in matters of religion. From this arises the right to religious freedom in society, in virtue of which men are able to practice their religion privately and publicly, and not be hindered therefrom by any force. This religious freedom demands that in human society the necessary conditions are brought about, in which everyone, both individually and gathered together in religious assemblies, may freely and completely respond to their divine calling" (n. 26).[20]

Negatively: "By religious freedom man is in no way emancipated from God's power, as though it were possible for him to give equal value to the false and the true, or as though he were absolved from all obligations toward the supreme deity, or as though it were not his duty to form for himself a right conscience in matters of religion, or as though he might arbitrarily decide for himself whether, and in what religion, he would serve God" (n. 26).

In the former draft, the basis of religious freedom as a universal right is the respect due to the "sincere conscience". Man has the duty to form his conscience according to the wisdom available to him, and a conscience thus formed is sincere *(recta)*, whether it be conformed to objective truth *(vera)* or not *(erronea)*. But the objections raised against such a basis were these: The respect due to the sincere though erroneous conscience is a form of tolerance or generosity and cannot be equated with the respect due to the sincere and

---

[20] The numbering of the paragraphs is nn. 25–31, since the schema is an appendix to the *Decree on Ecumenism*. The introduction (n. 25) states that the consideration of religious freedom is an "absolutely necessary condition for any possible ecumenical dialogue".

true conscience. Does not the attempt to base religious freedom on the rights of the sincere conscience lead inevitably to a confusion between the objective and subjective orders?

Furthermore, can the right to religious freedom be claimed *only* by those who are "in good faith", and not also by those who, despite better knowledge, or for lack of effort to obtain it, do not profess the true religion? Can society in any way coerce those "in bad faith"? And what human agent can ever determine who is sincere, who insincere? Does not man in his ultimate decision in religious matters, whether he decides for the truth or deliberately rejects it, stand in ultimate relation to God, before whom he has to decide as a free being, independent of any external constraint? If this freedom were not recognized by human society, the danger would still prevail of confusing spiritual and secular power, the internal and external forum, civil legislation and moral obligation.

As a result of these quite legitimate questions to the former draft, the plea was for a basis of religious freedom as a universal principle which is based on the objective order and thus does not depend on the subjective dispositions of the person.

In the new draft, the right to freedom in religious matters is based on the Christian understanding of human existence. To be human means to be created in the image of God and to be called by him into holy fellowship with him. The foundation for religious freedom is precisely this *vocatio divina,* the call of God which goes out to every man and is the objective basis for his quest for transcendental truth and goodness:

"The call of God, which opens up and prescribes for man the path to God and the attainment of salvation in God, constitutes the human person's highest dignity. Therefore, in social intercourse, the freedom to follow this call constitutes at once the greatest and most peculiar good of each individual, and the basis and safeguard of all other freedoms, and therefore must be regarded as a true and strict right, and one to be observed toward all those with whom one is living" (n. 29).

2. More explicit indications about the importance of the objective truth of the divine law.

In order to exclude all danger of subjectivism and indifferentism, the draft clearly states that the "norm of this [divine] calling of man, as of his whole relationship with God, is the divine law, which is eternal, objective, absolute and universal. Every individual is therefore obliged to know this ordinance of God correctly and with all zeal so that he may freely conform himself to it" (n. 29). Thus, no man can claim a "right to freedom" in the face of God's truth for right living.

3. Explicit indications of the rights of religious groups.

Although the former text did not ignore the recognition of freedom for religious groups, the new draft is clearer: "The right to religious freedom which individual persons possess must also be acknowledged for religious groups." And for this reason: they are set up by the free will of men who are following their consciences. Moreover, the social nature and dignity of man require that he be able to live his religion in public.

The draft spells out the rights of these religious

bodies "to govern themselves by their own laws, to honor God in their worship, to assist their members in the practice of their religious life and sustain them with their doctrine, and to promote those institutions in which the members lend their mutual aid in ordering the activities of life in accordance with their religious principles" (n. 30).

4. *An explanation of when and to what degree it is permissible to set certain limits to the external exercise of religious freedom.*

"On account of man's social nature, the exercise of rights in religious matters is limited and must not exceed that measure without which it would really be impossible to have a society of men who, being endowed with free will and infected with the consequences of original sin, are capable of error. This exercise of rights cannot legitimately be limited except insofar as it is gravely contrary to the very purpose of society, which consists in the aggregate of those conditions of social life in which men can more fully and more readily attain to their perfection, and at the same time faithfully observe the inalienable rights given by God to all men in common" (n. 29).

In order to avoid all misunderstanding the same principle is repeated in another form: "If it is proven that in the course of religious activity perverse practices occur which are clearly offensive to the dignity of the human person and the rights of others, then those who govern the people (*populorum rectores*) must prudently prevent this" (n. 29). At the same time, however, the incompetence of the State authority in religious matters is stressed: it has "no direct power or competence to determine or regulate the relations of citizens with their creator and savior, and therefore they cannot subordinate religious communities to the government's temporal purposes" (n. 30).

The draft explicitly distinguishes between "the right to work for the sincere and honest propagation or proclamation of religion", and the abuse of this right by " 'proselytism', which involves the use of improper and dishonest means" (n. 30).

5. *Further arguments to support the thesis.*

Lest the thesis of the document appear to be based exclusively on "ideals" of the theological order, the draft concludes with brief mention of arguments drawn from the experience of the modern world.

"It is clearly evident that the human race day by day is becoming more united, that the relations binding together men of different cultures and religions are becoming more closely knit; that among all people the consciousness of one's own responsibility is increasing, that government, on account of the juridical structure of its system, is incapable of passing judgment as to the truth in matters of religion. Peaceful coexistence and a just concord in the human family today are for the most part unrealizable unless God's supreme and most holy calling, and man's noble right and duty to lead a religious life freely in society, are respected and observed everywhere in the world" (n. 31).

The Council fathers debated the text on September 23, 24, 25 and 28. In general, nineteen speeches were against the draft, twenty-three in favor.[21]

---

[21] The stark figure is misleading. Those who strongly op-

From the discussions, and also from written suggestions, the mind of the Council was crystallizing into clear patterns. Every intervention favored "religious freedom", but its meaning and limitations revealed the different theological convictions on the relation between spiritual and temporal authority, as well as divergent legal traditions of Church-State relations in various countries: e.g., between the "American experience", the Spanish tradition, the Christian minority status in Africa and Asia and the oppressed Church in most socialist countries.

The radical opponents agreed that a Declaration on the subject was urgent in view of the persecution of the Church in the Communist countries. One must vindicate the rights of the Church—that is, the rights of the one true religion. But this vindication must be done in such a way as not to give unlimited freedom to the erring conscience; otherwise, the very foundations of the Catholic edifice would be thereby threatened and the "religious unity of entire Catholic nations" endangered. Objectively, no religious doctrine other than Roman Catholic had the right to propagation, since this went against the will of Christ. To grant equal rights to religious freedom for all religious groups was to judge their equal validity before God and men. Or, if one wanted to state anything about the free activity of an erring conscience and non-Catholic communities, the more exact word to use is "tolerance", not "freedom". One tolerates an evil —not approves it—in order to avoid a greater evil to the common good of the nation.

---

posed spoke in their own name, and their geographical representation was limited (thirteen were Italian or Spanish). Of those who spoke favorably, eight represented large numbers of fathers who were geographically scattered, four in the name of over seventy fathers.

The Secretariat document, continued the opponents, cannot be reconciled with papal teaching. From Gregory XVI to Pius XII (Pope John is never cited!), three fundamental truths are obvious: (1) The rights of the Church are not the same before civil power as those of other religions; (2) The State can and should acknowledge the true religion and its unique rights; (3) There should not be complete separation between Church and State, but *concordia;* and thus the State can sometimes tolerate the cult and propagation of another religion for the sake of the common good.[22]

The Secretariat's responses to these radical but traditional objections had been foreseen and were already contained in its official reports. But, it seemed, the efforts were insufficient.

A compromise proposition was surprisingly proposed by Cardinal Ritter (St. Louis). Acceptance of the main principles of the Declaration did not necessarily mean acceptance of the reasons for it. A simple statement could be worked out without making any attempt to justify it. Soon afterward, both Cardinal Ottaviani and Archbishop Parente (second to the cardinal in the Holy Office) seconded the American prelate's proposal, but nothing came of it. For the majority, there was still not enough evidence of a stalemate, and therefore no need of compromise solutions.[23]

---

[22] In the third session the radical minority of the Council began to organize itself into a group called *Coetus internationalis patrum.* This group efficiently printed and distributed background papers, and in the fourth session even worked out suggested *modi* to be signed by individual fathers if they wished. The three points above are found in a fourth session document of the Coetus, *Doctrina Romanorum Pontificum collata cun doctrina contenta in schemate declarationis de libertate religiosa.*

[23] In the name of seventy bishops (the entire hierarchy of

Among the supporters of the present document there still remained differing opinions concerning the methodology and focus of argument.

One group, led primarily by French bishops, insisted on a predominantly theological statement, "a prophetic text which shows forth the mysterious respect of God for the liberty of men whom he has created and developed in grace". With such an approach, the Declaration would be a powerful way of announcing the Good News to the world, the Good News that man is destined to a truth that transcends him and to a friendship that passes beyond the limitations of this life.

A more numerous group, however, pressed for a document that could be addressed to all men and be understood by legislators and governments, much in the style of Pope John's *Pacem in terris*. It should emphasize the juridical notion—the right of the person and of communities to social and civil freedom in matters religious. Such a document would be in harmony with the Charter on Human Rights of the United Nations.[24] Nevertheless, the

England and Wales, and many from Scotland, Ireland, Australia, New Zealand, France and Belgium), Cardinal John Heenan (Westminster) forcefully told the Council at the end of the religious freedom discussion (Sept. 28): "It has been said in this debate that only the principles need be set down and that no attempt should be made to explain the underlying Catholic doctrine. This argument seems to me faulty. In a pastoral document of this kind it is necessary to give some indication of the methods by which we have reached our conclusions. This at least is certain: many outside the Church hold that Catholics do not sincerely believe in religious freedom. Let us declare to the whole world, once and for all, our heartfelt belief as Catholics in the full liberty of all the sons of God." Cf. full text in *English Bishops at the Council: Third Session*, ed. Derek Worlock (London: Burns & Oates, 1965), pp. 98–100.

24 Insisting on this was Bishop Smijan Čekada (Skoplje, Yugoslavia). He further suggested that a commission prepare a

validity of this juridical notion would be established by a convergence of theological and ethical, as well as of political and legal, arguments.

Thus, the document would be indeed pastoral, but its content would be based on three doctrinal tenets: the ethical doctrine of religious freedom as a human right; a political doctrine with regard to the function and limits of government in religious matters; the theological doctrine of the freedom of the Church as the fundamental principle in what concerns the relations between the Church and the socio-political order.[25]

This latter judgment would dominate over all further redrafting.[26]

Perhaps the most influential supporting speech was that of titular Bishop Carlo Colombo. Because he is the personal theological advisor to Pope Paul, the fathers suspected a higher head reading approvingly over the bishop's shoulder.

"Unless we have this Declaration, there can be no dialogue with the modern world," claimed Bishop Colombo; the document was a prerequisite

---

text that, with conciliar backing, could be sent directly to the United Nations.

[25] John Courtney Murray, S.J., in his introduction to the Declaration, *The Documents of Vatican II,* ed. Walter M. Abbott, S.J. (New York: Guild, America, and Association Presses, 1966), pp. 672–673.

[26] Mention should be made of the help which the Secretariat now enlisted from the noted American theologian, Fr. John Courtney Murray, S.J., and from Msgr. Pietro Pavan, a chief drafter of *Pacem in terris*. Chiefly through the influence of these two men, the redrafting could be expertly shifted in its argument and narrowed in its scope. Fr. Murray had not worked on the second session draft, although he did prepare a background paper which helped shape the content of Bishop de Smedt's first *relatio* to the Council. The American Jesuit started to work directly on the schema only during the third session.

for Schema XIII concerning the relationship of the Church to the world of today.

He accordingly called for a careful working out of three bases for religious freedom. Two bases are of the natural order: (1) man has a natural right to the search for truth, especially religious truth,[27] and thus the right to investigation and dialogue in the quest; (2) man has the right to follow his conscience in the religious as in the other areas of his life.

The third basis is supernatural in nature: the relationship between the freedom of the believer and the supernatural character of Christian faith. "There is no religious act which is not free." And to avoid any hint of subjectivism or relativism, it should be explicitly mentioned that every man has the duty to seek the truth with all available and suitable means. For the Catholic the teaching authority of the Church is one of these means. Furthermore, revealed truth has value for every society, even for the natural, human life.

The present draft, of course, rejected none of these principles, but as they were only implied, a new draft should state them more explicitly. The Secretariat would do just that.

The exacting work of redrafting had hardly begun when, in early October, a serious crisis occurred. It proved to be shortlived. The Secretary General of the Council had written Cardinal Bea's group of "a desire of the Holy Father that the [religious freedom] text be reconsidered and reworked" by a special mixed commission.[28] The

---

27 He quoted directly from a Council speech which Cardinal Montini had delivered during the first session.

28 Such a commission had been suggested on the Council

same letter gave the names of four non-Secretariat members; three were prelates noted for their opposition to the basic argument of the present draft. Bishop Carlo Colombo was the fourth.

Such an arrangement was opposed to the conciliar rules: texts presented for discussion by a commission remain within that commission's competency right up to final promulgation unless the Council fathers themselves vote otherwise. Did the pope wish to overrule this normal procedure? News of the letter's demands quickly reached the bishops and the press (and many of the bishops through the press!). The counter-opposition was a petition sent to Pope Paul by fourteen cardinals. They pleaded for normal conciliar procedure. "In such an important matter," they wrote, "any appearance of a violation of the rules of the Council and its freedom would be extremely prejudicial to the whole Church in the light of world opinion." It is not yet known how detailed was the pope's original desire. In any case, his answer to the cardinals' petition outlined future procedure: the draft would remain under the sole jurisdiction of the Unity Secretariat; a special commission of ten would merely offer suggestions.

Redrafting resumed, based mainly upon the 140 submitted interventions. The Secretariat narrowed the broad theme of religious freedom down to the specific juridical notion and considerably enlarged the treatment of this refinement.

Before its official printing, the text passed through three tests: the mixed commission appointed by the pope (nine approvals, one against); the Theological Commission (twelve approvals, nine reserved approvals, six against); and, after

floor by Cardinal F. Quiroga y Palacios (Santiago de Compostela, Spain) on Sept. 23.

weighing the objections, the Unity Secretariat (unanimous).

The revised text was distributed to the Council fathers on Tuesday, November 17, only four days before the end of the third session. On the same day the Secretary General announced that the Council would vote section by section on the draft on the next Thursday. In the meantime, a small, unknown number petitioned the governing authorities for a postponement of both discussion and voting. The text, they claimed, was altered so much that it should be considered as a new text, and there was no time left for proper study. They were within their rights so to petition.[29]

On Wednesday the fathers were asked to prepare themselves for a preliminary vote on the next day to decide if they would vote at all. But on Thursday the Council moderators decided to postpone any kind of vote. The majority was shocked. It wanted the vote—which it predicted would be very favorable—on at least the suitability of the draft as a basis of future revision. Such a vote would both facilitate the work of redrafting before the fourth and final session and ease the growing anxiety of public opinion over the persistent refusal to face up to an honest application of the *Decree on Ecumenism* which was soon to be promulgated at the end of the third session. Some 500 bishops petitioned the Holy Father that "a vote on the *Declaration on Religious Freedom* be taken be-

---

29 In the *Ordo Concilii*, Art. 30, par. 2: "The schemata of decrees and canons, as well as all texts to be approved, must be distributed to the fathers in such a way as to permit them adequate time to consider them for their judgments and decisions on their vote." Art. 35: "The general congregations, after hearing the report of the *relator*, shall examine the parts of every amended text one by one and then approve them or not."

fore the end of this session of the Council, lest the confidence of the world, both Christian and non-Christian, be lost".

But the pope upheld the decision to postpone. The rules of the Council must be observed. One should respect "the freedom of those fathers, for whom it is a matter of utmost concern that a schema of such great importance be properly and thoroughly examined and evaluated". The Holy Father guaranteed that the document would be treated at the fourth session, "and, if possible, before all other schemata". The promise was carried out.

The Text

The general approach, content and method of the third major draft would in fact remain that of the subsequent drafts and of the final, promulgated Declaration. One therefore need not give details here, as has been done for the previous drafts. Subsequent clarifications, removal or additions of important passages can best be understood by starting from the final text and moving backwards by means of footnotes.

The general *approach* is now an address to all men, whether Christian or not. The *subject* is very specific: the right of the person and of religious groups to social and civil freedom in religious matters. There is a twofold civic "freedom" rooted in the very dignity of the human person; no man is to be forcibly constrained to act against his conscience, and no man is to be forcibly restrained from acting according to his conscience unless such exercise seriously disturbs the public peace, violates public morality or results in infringement on the rights of others. The *method* is to resolve this juridical, political and ethical question by rational arguments confirmed by experience in the secular world. Truth is the foundation of religious freedom, not the truth of what man believes but of what he is—a human person blessed with free choice. Religious freedom is not simply a good for the individual; it is a good for society itself and, as such, must be guaranteed and fostered by public authorities. Besides rational arguments, divine revelation can be used, but biblical texts only show the "roots" of religious freedom; they do not "prove" civil and social immunity from coercion.

Once more began the weary work of rewriting during the winter months. There had been 218 written interventions turned in, 12 of which were in the name of several fathers. The Secretariat once more asked the Theological Commission for the individual opinions of its members. Then there was still further revision. The Coordinating Commission decided to detach the Declaration completely from *De Oecumenismo,* since the first three chapters had already been promulgated at the end of the third session.

The bishops received the new text in June, 1965.[30] In the same booklet was a dense twenty-

---

30 In his general audience of June 28, Pope Paul said that the words of Christ, "Come to me", are at the center of the "great problem of religious freedom". Christ "produces a moral obligation for those who receive the invitation, a saving obligation. But it does not take away the physical liberty of man who must consciously decide for himself about his destiny and his relations with God. . . . There exists an order to instruct and to instruct oneself. There exists a supreme responsibility regarding the religious problem to which we must

five page report which presented the major observations of the bishops and then outlined the methods and principles of the new Declaration. This latter part is so important for an understanding of the Secretariat's work and approach to persistent major objections that its adapted version is here presented in Appendix II, pp. 109-130.

---

and can respond in one way only—freely, that is, through and with love, not through force. Christianity is love" *(L'Osservatore Romano,* June 29, 1965).

FOURTH SESSION
1965

Discussion on the new religious freedom draft opened the fourth session, September 15-22. Sixty-four fathers spoke.

The majority was reaching its consensus. In the name of 82 Brazilian bishops, Cardinal Agnelo Rossi (São Paulo) praised the new draft "as a synthesis, and for its depth and opportuneness". Bishop John Gran (Oslo) stressed "the great source of scandal" to the Scandinavians "should this Council not speak openly and unambiguously on this topic". He added: "We are a small flock, and yet we enjoy great liberty. Daily we see our religious liberty defended by non-Catholic civil leaders, not because they agree with us in all things, but because of our human dignity." The U.S. speakers (Cardinals Cushing, Ritter, Shehan and Spellman, Archbishop Hallinan of Atlanta and Bishop Charles Maloney of Louisville) all understandably pressed for quick approval.

Three French bishops (Léon Elchinger of Strasbourg, Jean Sauvage of Annecy and Alfred Ancel of Lyons—the last spoke for over 100 bishops) who previously had been leading the plea for a primarily theological statement on Christian freedom now conceded. Bishop Sauvage said that with the narrowing of the theme to social and civil rights, the Council "shall propose a universal minimum source of freedom that can be accepted by everyone and shall avoid the broad questions of the relations between Church and State and of Christian freedom".

47

The "signs of the times" were revealing the necessity of the Church's abandoning many of its past habits and methods. Cardinal Josef Cardijn concluded from his "almost sixty years of priestly apostolate for the youth and workers in all parts of the world": "To fulfill its mission, the Church can no longer rely on the help of temporal powers (political, economic, or cultural), but only on the strength of the Word of God, evangelical poverty, the purity of its witness as seen in the life of the laity, and the benevolence of the people among whom it wishes to live. This benevolence is nothing other than religious freedom." Cardinal Paul Silva Henriquez (Santiago, Chile) warned against the Church's excessive confidence in riches, political authority or any means which does not respect the human person: "Care should be taken not only as regards those outside our religion, but also for our own members, that no coercion of any kind—political, economic, sociological or psychological—be used to promote the faith."

As a remarkable moving commentary to the Chilean prelate's remarks, Cardinal Josef Beran (Prague) spoke humbly from his Czechoslovakian experience (only seven months before he had been released from long years of prison and house arrest) : "From the very moment when freedom of conscience was radically restricted in my country, I was witness not only to the grave dangers to the faith, but also to the serious temptations to hypocrisy and other moral vices that the oppression of conscience brought in its wake. Experience teaches that oppression of conscience, not only when it is to the detriment of the true religion, but even when it is intended or pretended to be for the good of the true faith, is morally pernicious.

"Thus the Church in my country now seems to be making painful expiation for the sins committed in the past against freedom of conscience in the name of the Church, such as the burning of John Hus and the forced re-Catholicizing of the majority of the Bohemian people. By such acts the civil authorities, wishing or pretending to serve the Church, in fact wounded it. This 'trauma' left hidden in the heart of the people was an impediment to spiritual progress and gave to the enemies of the Church easy material for agitation.

"History warns us to declare the principles of religious freedom and freedom of conscience clearly and without restriction. If this is done, and in a spirit of penance for past sins, the moral authority of the Church and of the Council will be increased, especially on behalf of those suffering religious persecution. Those who oppress freedom of conscience to the detriment of the Church will be isolated before all men of goodwill. We should in no way diminish the force of this Declaration, and at its conclusion should be added a plea to all governments to fully recognize freedom of conscience and to cease from any oppression of it, to free incarcerated priests and laity, to permit autonomy of the Churches and free communication with the See of Peter, to remove obstacles preventing youths from embracing the priesthood and religious life, et cetera."

Irritation was expressed over a new passage on the legitimate, privileged establishment of one religion without injuring the religious rights of others.[31] Many, especially Cardinals Bernard Alfrink (Utrecht), Joseph Frings (Cologne), Franjo Šeper (Zagreb, Yugoslavia) and Agnelo Rossi

---

[31] Cf. n. 6, footnote 15, pp. 75-76.

(São Paulo), would accept at the most the theoretical possibility, but refused categorically to approve each and every *de facto* Church-State situation. Others were more critical. Archbishop Duraisamy Lourdusamy (Bangalore, India) said that in a pluralistic and shrinking world, such special recognition is "more harmful than helpful to the cause of the privileged religion itself", and that in mission countries "the condition of Catholics would become deplorable if such recognition were accorded to non-Christian religions". The same point was registered by Bishop Michael Doumith (Sarba, Lebanon), in the name of 70 fathers from the Middle East, Africa and Asia: "Generally, among non-Christians the religious law of the confessional State is the source of all law, and thus the non-believers suffer grave discrimination. . . . Since careful distinctions have to be made about different types of confessional States, it is better that the whole issue be dropped." Maronite Archbishop Ignace Ziade (Beirut, Lebanon) wanted the subject dropped because he held that special recognition in fact contradicts religious freedom.

No matter how technically precise the document was or could become, there were still misgivings and fears. Would not some well-financed denominational groups use the Declaration to support the exploitation of peoples unprepared socially and educationally to distinguish the wheat of the Christian witness from the chaff of sectarian proselytism? And Catholics themselves, would not some use the document—perhaps without reading it!—in order to isolate conscience from the Christ-given authority of the Church and identify the voice of conscience with personal values rather than divine imperatives or objective considerations which transcend personal crises?

A vast majority of the supporters of the proposed theses in the schema still pressed for a clearer distinction between the spiritual order of man's relations to truth and Truth, and the social and political order of man's relations to other men and to government (the demand, for example, of Cardinal Giovanni Urbani and 32 Italian bishops). These bishops requested: (1) the Catholic belief in the uniqueness of the Church and its universal mission; (2) the demands of truth upon man's search for it, especially the demands of truth as proclaimed by the magisterium of the Church upon those who so believe in its specific religious teaching authority; (3) the "development", not contradiction, of previous papal teaching.

All three points were eventually introduced, although there would be disagreement as to their proper location and exact phrasing (cf. nn. 1-2).

The "radical opposition" still was strong in the discussions. It still would not accept the Secretariat's answers to its main objections (cf. Appendix II, pp. 120-124): (1) the Declaration vindicated religious freedom not only for the Roman Catholic Church, but for all religions, and for all consciences, whether "true" or "false". But "only the Church has the right to freedom", declared Archbishop Marcel Lefebvre, C.Sp.S. And Cardinal Ottaviani stated: "The true and the false are not equal and cannot enjoy the same rights";[32] (2) the Declara-

---

[32] On Sept. 17, Bishop Charles Maloney (Louisville, Ky.) offered what he called "a charitably presented *ad hominem* argument": "Certainly contradictory things have been said in this discussion, and so some of them must be erroneous. By what right have those who erred spoken? Not by right of truth, but by right of their persons as Council fathers, i.e., by reason of the faculty of freedom exercised without coercion. So also the right to religious freedom is the right of a person, even an erring person."

tion contradicts past papal statements. Again Archbishop Lefebvre declared: "The concept of liberty proposed by the schema comes neither from the Church nor from tradition, but from 18th-century philosophers: Hobbes, Rousseau, Locke. It was taken over by Lamennais and condemned by several popes."

Archbishop Gregorio Modrego y Casáus (Barcelona) questioned authentic doctrinal development by using the argument from Church practice. Popes, he said, "often ordered or asked governments in Catholic societies not to grant or recognize the civil right of non-Catholics to profess publicly or to propagate their faiths". Although much against the schema, Cardinal Michael Browne (Roman Curia) contradicted the Spanish prelate. The doctrine of the Roman pontiffs, he claimed, intended that in Catholic States the public authority treat non-Catholics equally, justly and benignly.

A few bishops still doubted the maturity of the schema's theme. The doctrine is based on rather recent studies concerning the origin of personal and social rights and the relation of the State to religion, but these studies do not seem sufficiently mature to be the firm foundation for a conciliar text (Bishop Paolo Muñoz Vega of Quito, Equador). Bishop John Baptist Velasco (Philippines), who thought the schema completely unacceptable, bluntly said: "The writers of the draft may think that I do not understand or interpret it correctly; even if this were so—after two years of studying and listening to the opinions of experts in theology and pastoral work—how could we expect our faithful and the people of the whole world to understand this schema?"

Evaluating these radical objections, the Secretariat was convinced that the document could only force an either-or vote. Some placating phrases would be introduced, but compromise theses would be impossible.[33]

Just how strong was this minority that wanted a radically different approach? Since there had never been an initial vote of previous drafts, both optimists and pessimists guessed publicly. The Secretariat was determined to flush out the exact number before its work of rewriting (or as Bishop de Smedt wryly put it, the Secretariat's re-re-rewriting). In a closed meeting (September 19), the conciliar governing authorities voted down the Secretariat's request for a preliminary vote. The vote was considered unnecessary. Pope Paul judged otherwise and directly intervened.[34]

On September 21, the General Secretary placed the question before the fathers: "Does it please the fathers that the amended text on religious freedom should be adopted as the basis of a definitive Declaration which will be further perfected according to the Catholic doctrine on the true religion and according to the amendment proposed by the fathers, in order to be submitted for their approbation according to the Council's rules?" The result: 1,997 voted *placet* (yes), 224 *non placet* (no). Thus, 88% were in favor of the document. The major

---

[33] For example, many opponents asked that the right be considered a positive civil right—that is, for the sake of the common good, government *grants* its citizenry the right to immunity from coercion. But the Declaration insists that the right is inherent in the person and that the government is to *acknowledge* this inherent right. The former opinion, stated the Secretariat's October *relatio*, goes against the substance of the Declaration, and therefore cannot be accepted. It's either-or.

[34] One of the reasons: the obvious bad effect of another postponement on public opinion shortly before the pope's visit to the United Nations (Oct. 4).

juridical and psychological obstacle had been hurdled.

Bishop de Smedt returned to the floor on October 10. He apologized to the Council for fear of boring it with the sixth official report and draft within three sessions. He asked the bishops to study the draft, then vote and turn in their suggested corrections. The fathers answered generously (October 26-27). Over 2,000 amendments, many of them repetitious, were analyzed by the Secretariat. It determined which were to be incorporated into the text.[35] On November 19, the bishops approved all of the new changes, although there was still a minority of 249 fathers who voted against the text as a whole. This number dwindled to 70 at the final vote, on December 7, with 2,308 *placets* and 8 null.

On the same day, Pope Paul VI, "together with the fathers of the sacred Council", issued the *Declaration on Religious Freedom*. Thus, in the words of Fr. J. C. Murray, "the text was flung into a pool whose shores are wide as the universal Church. The ripples will run far".

---

[35] This writer worked closely on three conciliar documents. He can vouch for the exhausting pressure of such work. Even after the hours and hours spent in cataloguing and analyzing amendments (and so many of them written by non-Spencerian hands), 80% of the time was needed for the writing of the official justification for the *non*-acceptance of hundreds of submitted *modi* (65 pages for *De libertate religiosa*. Then followed the proofreading of dense Latin galleys. One co-worker exclaimed: "Slaves to religious liberty!"

Study-Club Questions

1. What commission was entrusted with preparing material on religious freedom for discussion at Vatican Council II?

2. Enumerate some of the alternative approaches to this question which the members of the Secretariat and its subcommission considered.

3. Did the majority of the Council fathers reach a consensus as to the most effective way of presenting the Catholic position on religious freedom?

4. What other Council schema, in its preparatory draft, contained contradictions of the statement on religious freedom?

5. What action was taken on the religious freedom document in the first session of the Council?

6. What eventually became the main support of the document on religious freedom?

7. What are the two different meanings of *conscientia recta* in theological tradition?

8. How many U.S. bishops were members of the Secretariat for Promoting Christian Unity during preparations for the Council and during its first session?

9. What had been the role of the U.S. bishops with respect to religious freedom and the Church-State question at Vatican Council I?

10. Who is obliged to acknowledge and respect men's right to religious freedom?

11. Name some of the ways in which the right to religious freedom may be infringed.

12. What are the meanings that one should be careful not to attach to the expression "religious freedom"?

13. What Council document is most closely related to the *Declaration on Religious Freedom?*

14. Why must we respect the freedom of each man's personal conscience?

15. To whom must the right to the free exercise of religion in society be extended?

16. Is it ever permissible to set limits to the external exercise of religious freedom?

17. Explain the relevance of Pope Paul's statement that one should respect "the freedom of those fathers for whom it is a matter of utmost concern that a schema of such great importance be properly and thoroughly examined and evaluated".

18. Discuss the positive and negative norms contained in the final draft of the document on religious freedom.

19. How does Pope Paul's statement that Christ produces a moral and saving obligation for those who receive the invitation of faith relate to the problem of religious freedom?

20. How did the remarks of Cardinal Beran of Prague contribute importantly to the Council's discussion of the religious freedom issue?

21. What were the implications of the "confessional State" for the Council discussion?

22. Do you think the Council's *Declaration on Reli-*

gious Freedom will tempt Catholics to disregard the Church's authority?

23. What was the argument presented by Auxiliary Bishop Charles Maloney of Louisville?

24. Why was it particularly surprising that Cardinal Browne contradicted Archbishop Modrego y Casáus of Barcelona?

25. When did the Council fathers vote on the *Declaration on Religious Freedom,* and what was the outcome?

OUTLINE OF THE DECLARATION

The Introduction (n. 1) reads the "signs of the times" concerning the free exercise of religion in society, and expresses the desire of Vatican Council II to develop recent papal doctrine on the inviolable rights of the human person and on the constitutional order of society.

The general principle of religious freedom is then stated: the right to freedom from coercion in religious matters; this right is based on the dignity of the human person (n. 2). The rational arguments are then presented (n. 3). This right to social and civil freedom applies not only to individuals but also to religious bodies (n. 4), with special mention of the family (n. 5). Such inviolable rights are to be protected and promoted by government (n. 6), which, in turn, defends its citizens against possible abuses on the pretext of freedom of religion (n. 7). Precisely because of the grandeur of this sacred right, everyone should help form each other to become lovers of true freedom and to exercise their freedom responsibly (n. 8).

This general principle has its roots in the revealed Word of God (nn. 9-14). Religious freedom is consonant with the freedom of the act of Christian faith (n. 10). This can be shown by the way Christ and his apostles acted toward others (n. 11). The Church should follow in the same way (n. 12), and claim for itself the right to enjoy that full measure of freedom which its care for the salvation of men requires (n. 13), a care which the Catholic faithful must confidently and courageously carry out with holy, evangelical means, and only with such means (n. 14) .

The Council regrets the present violation of authentic religious freedom, and it pleads for effective constitutional guarantees of that freedom everywhere in order that peace and harmony may be established and maintained within the whole of mankind (n. 15) .

De Libertate Religiosa

DECLARATION
ON
RELIGIOUS FREEDOM
OF
VATICAN COUNCIL II

Promulgated by Pope Paul VI
December 7, 1965

The basic translation of the Declaration here published is that endorsed by the bishops of the United States at the close of the fourth Council session (December, 1965). However, for greater accuracy and clarity, several changes have been introduced by Fr. Thomas F. Stransky, C.S.P.

In this translation the official notes of the Declaration, except for the lengthy one in n. 10, have been incorporated within the text itself. The explanatory footnotes are those of the commentator.

NOTE: References to the last four versions of the Declaration are by letter:

(A) Revision distributed at the end of the third session (Nov. 19, 1964).

(B) Revision based on written suggestions after the third session and mailed to the Council fathers during the summer of 1965.

(C) Revision based on the conciliar discussion at the fourth session (Sept. 1965) and distributed in the Council (Oct. 10).

(D) Revision which includes the amendments (*modi*) accepted by the Secretariat and distributed to the fathers in mid-November.

The paragraph titles are not in the text promulgated but are taken from the draft text (D) which received the Council's preliminary approval on November 19, 1965.

PAUL BISHOP

SERVANT OF THE SERVANTS OF GOD
TOGETHER WITH THE FATHERS OF THE SACRED COUNCIL
COMMITS TO PERMANENT RECORD

DECLARATION
ON
RELIGIOUS FREEDOM

ON THE RIGHT OF THE PERSON
AND OF COMMUNITIES TO SOCIAL AND
CIVIL FREEDOM IN RELIGIOUS MATTERS [1]

Introduction[2]

1. Contemporary man is becoming more deeply conscious of the dignity of the human person (cf. John XXIII, Encyclical Letter *Pacem in terris,* April 11, 1963: *A.A.S.* 55 [1963], p. 279; *ibid.,* p. 265; Pius XII, Radio Message of Dec. 24, 1944: *A.A.S.* 37 [1945], p. 14). There is an increase of those who de-

---

[1] The official subtitle of the Declaration. It immediately limits the subject: 1) not the relation of man to truth or to God, but the relations between people in human and civic society; 2) not the relations between the faithful and Church authorities, but the relations of men to other men, to human communities and to government.

The official Latin title of the Declaration is its first three words: *Dignitas humanae personae.*

[2] Mostly at the suggestion of French-speaking bishops (cf. above, pp. 39 and 114), in the preparation of (B) a long preface was composed which presented the divine pedagogy in salvation history leading men toward human freedom and personhood. But the majority of the Unity Secretariat voted that such a richly theological preface would not go well with the highly rational approach of the first part of the draft. The contents of the preface were then drastically reduced and introduced into the second part of the Declaration.

mand that in his actions man should act on his own judgment, that he should enjoy and make use of a responsible freedom, not driven by coercion but motivated by a sense of duty. At the same time, they demand constitutional limitation of the powers of government in order to prevent encroachment on the rightful freedom of the person and of associations. This demand for freedom in human society chiefly concerns the sphere of man's spiritual values. It regards primarily the free exercise of religion in society.

This Vatican Council takes careful note of these spiritual aspirations. It proposes to declare to what extent they are in accord with truth and justice. To this end, it searches into the sacred tradition and teaching of the Church—the treasury out of which the Church continually brings forth new things ever in harmony with the old.

First,[3] the Council professes its belief that God himself has made known to mankind the way in which men are to serve him and thus be saved in Christ and come to blessedness. We believe that this one true religion subsists in the Catholic and apostolic Church[4] to which the Lord Jesus entrusted

---

[3] This strong profession of Catholic belief was introduced after the fourth session discussion (cf. above, p. 51): (1) the uniqueness of the Church and its universal mission (the former text [B] stated that "the meaning of religious freedom leaves intact the Catholic doctrine of the one true religion and the one Church of Christ", but the fathers judged this too weak) ; (2) the demands of religious truth upon men; (3) the development of papal teaching. After (C) there were conciliar complaints about placing these points in the introduction. However, the drafters did so in order to state immediately the distinction between the spiritual order and the social and political order before the text proceeded with the specific treatment of the latter.

[4] The *Constitution on the Church* adds: ". . . which is governed by the successor of Peter and by bishops in com-

the task of spreading this religion abroad among all men. Thus he spoke to the apostles: "Go, therefore, and make disciples of all nations, baptizing them in the name of the Father and of the Son and of the Holy Spirit, teaching them to observe all things whatsoever I have enjoined upon you" (Mt. 28, 19-20). On their part, all men are bound to seek the truth, especially in what concerns God and his Church, and to embrace the truth they come to know, and to hold fast to it.

This Vatican Council likewise professes its belief that it is upon the human conscience that these obligations fall and exert their binding force. The only way truth can impose itself is by the force of its own gentle but powerful influence on the mind of man. Religious freedom, in turn, which men demand as necessary to fulfill their duty to worship God, has to do with immunity from coercion in civil society. Therefore, it leaves untouched traditional Catholic doctrine on the moral duty of men and societies toward the true religion and toward the one Church of Christ.

Over and above all this, the Council in its treatment of religious freedom intends to develop the teaching of recent popes on the inviolable rights of the human person and the constitutional ordering of society.[5]

---

munion with him" (n. 8). On the precise meaning and ecumenical significance of the word *subsist* (not *is*), cf. the commentary by Gregory Baum, O.S.A., *The Constitution on the Church* (Glen Rock, N.J.: Paulist Press, 1965), pp. 22–24. Also cf. Thomas F. Stransky, C.S.P., "The Decree on Ecumenism," in *Vatican II: An Interfaith Appraisal* (New York: Association Press, 1966).

5 How does one square the Declaration with 19th-century—not to mention medieval—pronouncements of the highest ecclessiastical authority? Bishop de Smedt tried to do so in his second session *relatio* (cf. Appendix I). The Secretariat also

I

The Principle of Religious Freedom in General

The Content and Basis of Religious Freedom

2. This Vatican Council declares that the human person has a right to religious freedom. This freedom means that all men are to be immune from coercion on the part of individuals, of social groups or of any human power, in such wise that in religious matters no one should be forced to act against his conscience or restrained from acting according to his conscience, whether privately or publicly, whether alone or in association with others, within due limits. The Council further declares that the right to religious freedom has its foundation in the very dignity of the human person, as this dignity is known through the revealed Word of God and by reason itself (cf. John XXIII, Encyclical Letter *Pacem in terris, op. cit.,* pp. 260-261; Pius XII, Radio Message of Dec. 24, 1942: *A.A.S.* 35 [1943], p. 19; Pius XI, Encyclical Letter

---

tried in a long (66 lines) paragraph in (A), but this attempt was discarded in all future drafts. At the fourth session Bishop de Smedt said that the difficult and complicated question of the doctrinal development of religious freedom is left to future scholars. He indicated "the substance of the problem": "Pontifical documents up to Leo XIII insisted more on the moral duties of government toward the true religion. The later popes, while holding on to this teaching, completed it by clarifying another duty of government—to observe the dignity of the human person in religious matters as a necessary element of the common good." Cf. the approach of J. C. Murray in Appendix IV. Most agree that the doctrinal development problem in regard to religious freedom will be a major burden for Vatican Council II scholars.

Mit brennender Sorge, March 14, 1937: *A.A.S.* 29 [1937], p. 160; Leo XIII, Encyclical Letter *Libertas praestantissimum,* June 20, 1888: *Acta Leonis XIII,* 8 [1888], pp. 237-238) . This right of the human peron to religious freedom must be so recognized in the constitutional law whereby society is governed that the right becomes a civil right.[6]

It is in keeping with their dignity as persons— that is, beings endowed with reason and free will and therefore privileged to bear personal responsibility—that all men should be at once driven by their own nature and also bound by a moral obligation to seek the truth, especially religious truth. They are also bound to cling to the truth, once it is known, and to order their whole lives in accord with the demands of truth.

However, men cannot fulfill this obligation in a manner which is in keeping with their own nature unless they enjoy immunity from external coercion as well as psychological freedom.[7] Therefore, the right to religious freedom has its foundation not in the subjective disposition of the person, but in his very nature. This means that the right to this immunity continues to exist even in those who do not live up to their obligation of seeking the

---

[6] This paragraph is the key declaration: the *nature* of religious freedom (the right of the person); the *object* (immunity from coercion); the *basis* (dignity of the human person) ; the *subject* (the individual and the religious group) .

[7] The *Constitution on the Church in the Modern World* introduces the impact of economic conditions on man's freedom: "A man can hardly arrive at the needed sense of responsibility unless his living conditions allow him to become conscious of his dignity and to rise to his destiny by spending himself for God and for others. But human freedom is often crippled when a man falls into extreme poverty, just as it withers when he indulges in too many of life's comforts and imprisons himself in a kind of splendid isolation" (n. 31).

truth and adhering to it,[8] and the exercise of this right is not to be impeded as long as just public order is maintained.

II

Religious Freedom and the Necessary Relation of Man to God

3. Further light is shed on the subject if one considers that the highest norm of human life is the divine law itself—eternal, objective and univer-

---

[8] Rejected are arguments based on the abstract notions of "truth" and "error" and/or on the "sincere" and "bad" conscience of citizens in relation to their civil right to religious freedom. The person—insofar as he is blessed with a good conscience or burdened with a bad one, conformed to truth or resting in error—is in another order, that of the spirit.

What about the "atheist"? Likewise, the spiritual problem of the atheist is distinct from his civil right to the same freedom as the believer enjoys. Some fathers wanted this stated clearly, but the drafters feared unnecessary opposition to such explicitness. (The W.C.C. New Delhi *Statement on Religious Liberty* speaks of the "right freely to maintain one's belief *or disbelief*". Cf. Appendix IV.) The civil right of the atheist thus remains implicit in the Declaration. But one reason for the consistent use of "freedom in religious matters (*in re religiosa*") and not *libertas religiosa* (which could be translated: "freedom in being religious") is to provide for the atheistic conviction, a conviction *in re religiosa*.

Of course, the atheist and a government with an atheistic policy should equally respect the civil rights of believers. But this is a more complicated question.

Furthermore, in *The Church in the Modern World* (nn. 19–21), Vatican Council II carefully avoids oversimplifying the problem of modern atheism and agnosticism, and rather attempts to analyze the complexities behind the phenomenon in their varied contemporary forms. The Council does not prejudge unbelievers, although it bluntly warns that those "who willfully shut out God from their hearts and try to dodge religious questions are not following the dictates of their conscience. Hence they are not free from blame" (n. 19). But this can also apply to the professed Christian who, in fact, is a "practical atheist".

sal. It is by this that God, in his own wisdom and love, orders, directs and governs the entire universe and all the ways of the human community. God has given man a share in his own law so that, under the gentle disposition of divine providence, he can come to perceive unchanging truth ever more fully. Thus every man has the duty, and therefore the right, to seek the truth in religious matters in order that, using appropriate means, he may prudently form for himself right and true judgments of conscience.

The search for truth, however, must be carried out by means proper to the dignity of the human person and his social nature. The inquiry is to be free and carried on with the aid of teaching or instruction, communications and dialogue.[9] By these means men explain to one another the truth they have discovered, or think they have discovered, in order to help one another in the quest for truth. But as the truth is discovered, it is by a personal assent that men are firmly to adhere to it.

A man's own conscience is the means whereby he perceives and acknowledges the imperatives of divine law. In all his activity he is bound to follow his conscience faithfully in order that he may come to God, the end and purpose of life. It follows that he is not to be forced to act in a manner contrary to his conscience. Nor is he to be restrained from acting in accordance with his conscience, especially in religious matters. The reason is that the exercise of religion, of its very nature, consists before all else in those voluntary and free internal acts whereby man sets the course of his life directly toward God. No merely human power can either command or prohibit acts of this kind (cf. John

---

[9] Cf. the speech of Bishop Colombo above, pp. 40-41.

XXIII, Encyclical Letter *Pacem in terris, op. cit.,* p. 270; Paul VI, Radio Message of Dec. 22, 1964: *A.A.S.* 57 [1965], pp. 181-182). However, the social nature of man itself requires that he should give external expression to those internal acts of religion, that he should participate with others in religious matters and that he should profess his religion in community.

Injury is therefore done to the human person and to the very order established by God for human life, if the free exercise of religion is denied in society when the just requirements of public order do not so require.

There is a further consideration. The religious acts whereby men, according to personal convictions, direct their lives to God—in private and in public—by their very nature transcend the order of terrestrial and temporal affairs. Government therefore ought indeed to take account of the religious life of the citizenry and show it favor, since the proper function of government is to care for the common temporal welfare. However, it would clearly transgress the limits set to its power, were it to presume to control or inhibit acts that are religious.[10]

---

[10] A delicately worded paragraph. In (B): "Civil authority goes beyond its limits when it interposes itself *(sese immisceat)* in matters which have to do with man's directing himself toward God." (C) was more specific, stating that government exceeds its limits when it "controls or inhibits *(vel impediat vel dirigat)* those things which by their nature transcend the earthly, temporal order". Standing by itself, this could mean the approval of an a-religious government. Thus, the approved amendment (D). No right resides in government to command or inhibit acts of religion, which by their nature lie beyond the reach of government. Nevertheless, it should favor *(favere)* the religious life of its citizenry—that is, "create conditions favorable to the fostering of religious life" (n. 6). The *favere* does not mean that civil authority may favor religious

The Freedom of Religious Groups

4. That freedom or immunity from coercion in religious matters which is the endowment of persons as individuals is also to be recognized as their right when they act in community. The community organization of religion is required by the social nature both of man and of religion itself.

Provided the just demands of public order are met, these religious groups have a right to immunity in order that they may govern themselves according to their own norms, honor the Supreme Being in public worship, assist their members in the practice of the religious life, strengthen them by instruction and promote institutions in which they may join together for the purpose of ordering their own lives according to their religious principles.

Religious groups also have the right not to be hindered, either by legal measures or by administrative action of the civil authority in the selection, training, appointment and transferral of their own ministers; [11] this also applies to contact with reli-

---

life, or a particular kind of it, in a manner contrary to the full freedom of all citizens (n. 6).

[11] The "appointment and transfer of ministers" was introduced (C) at the request of bishops who complained of government interference, including some "Catholic" governments. The *Decree on the Pastoral Office of Bishops in the Church* (n. 20) tries to correct the historical anomaly of some governments' "rights or privileges of election, nomination, presentation or designation for the office of bishop". The Council desires the cessation of these rights "in order to duly protect the freedom of the Church and to promote more suitably and efficiently the welfare of the faithful", and it

gious authorities and communities living in other parts of the world and to the erection of buildings for religious purposes, as well as to the acquisition and use of what funds or properties they need.

Religious communities have the further right not to be hindered in their public teaching and bearing witness to their faith by the spoken or written word. However, in spreading religious faith and in introducing religious practices, everyone should always refrain from any manner of action which might seem to carry a hint of coercion or any other form of dishonest or unworthy persuasion, especially when dealing with poor or uneducated people. Such a manner of action would have to be considered an abuse of one's own right and a violation of the right of others.[12]

---

gently asks the civil authorities concerned "to renounce voluntarily these rights and privileges which they now enjoy by reason of treaty or custom."

An extreme example: according to the Vatican–Spanish Concordat (1953), the Spanish government, in consultation with the Vatican Nuntio, draws up a list of six episcopal candidates, from which the Holy See, in turn, selects three. From these three the government names the bishop-to-be.

[12] One should distinguish between "witness" and "proselytism". For the Christian, witness is carried out by using only means which carry the power of the Word of God and respect the legitimate sensibilities of the other person (cf. *The Church in the Modern World*, n. 76). Proselytism is the corruption of religious witness by irreligious means: e.g., cajolery, bribery, undue pressure or intimidation—subtle or open—falsifying or oversimplifying the others' beliefs or practices, etc. Witness is the right of every religious group; proselytism is the right of none. Cf. below, Appendix IV.

(B) introduced, in the first sentence, after "written word": "provided that the legitimate demands of public order are not violated". But an accepted amendment (D) dropped the phrase and added the last sentence. The addition can cause legitimate questioning. If every form of proselytism is

In addition, it comes within the meaning of religious freedom that religious groups should not be prohibited from freely undertaking to show the special value of their teaching in what concerns the organization of society and inspires the whole of human activity. Finally, the social nature of man and the very nature of religion are the bases of the right by which men, when prompted by their own religious sense, may hold meetings freely and set up educational, cultural, charitable and social organizations.

The Religious Freedom of the Family

5. The family is a society which enjoys its own basic rights. As such it has the right freely to live its own domestic religious life under the guidance of parents. Parents, moreover, have the right to determine, according to their own religious beliefs, the kind of religious education that their children are to receive. The civil authority must therefore acknowledge the parents' right to make genuinely free choice of schools and of other means of education, and the use of this freedom of choice is not to be made a reason for imposing unjust burdens on parents, whether directly or indirectly. Moreover, the rights of parents are violated if their

---

a violation of the rights of others (*laesio iurium*), is this a violation of one's *civil* rights. If so, then any civil authority, because it has the "essential duty" to protect these rights (n. 6), could legally and coercively repress any form of proselytism. Would this not lead to abusive interference in religious matters by a government judging that some religious group is acting in an "unworthy way"? Cf. A. F. Carrillo de Albornoz, "The Ecumenical and World Significance of the Vatican Declaration on Religious Liberty," in *Ecumenical Review* (Jan. 1966), pp. 16–17.

children are forced to attend lessons or instruction which go against their religious beliefs, or if a single system of education which gives no place at all to religious formation is imposed upon all.[13]

The Care for Religious Freedom

6. The common welfare of society is the sum total of those conditions of social life which enable men to achieve a fuller measure of perfection with some relative ease. Because this common good consists mainly in the protection of the rights of —and in the performance of these duties by—the human person (cf. John XXIII, Encyclical Letter *Mater et Magistra,* May 15, 1961: *A.A.S.* 53 [1961], p. 417; *idem,* Encyclical Letter *Pacem in terris, op. cit.,* p. 273), the care for the right to religious freedom is the common responsibility of the whole citizenry, social groups, civil authorities, the Church and other religious communities. The individual responsibility of each of these will vary according to its duty toward the common welfare.

The protection and promotion of the inviolable rights of man are essential duties of any civil authority [14] (cf. John XXIII, Encyclical Letter

---

[13] There was some pressure for an explicit mention of the government's obligation to give financial support to Catholic schools. The suggestion was flatly rejected. A whole set of historical, social and civic circumstances determine what is a direct or indirect *unjust* burden. Cf. nn. 6–7 of *The Declaration on Christian Education,* with a commentary by Mark J. Hurley (Glen Rock, N.J.: Paulist Press, 1966), pp. 70–76.

The last sentence was introduced at the request of many fathers from Communist regimes (e.g., cf. the fourth session speech by Cardinal Joseph Slipyi of Lwow, Ukraine).

[14] The Declaration never uses the word State, but rather *potestas civilis* or *publica.* "State" would have stirred up the

Pacem in terris, op. cit., pp. 273-274; Pius XII, Radio Message of June 1, 1941: *A.A.S.* 33 [1941], p. 200). Therefore, government has an obligation to give effective protection to the religious freedom of all its citizens by just laws and by other appropriate means. Government is also to help create conditions favorable to the fostering of religious life in order that the citizens are really in a position to exercise their religious rights and to fulfill their religious duties, and also in order that society itself may enjoy the benefits of justice and peace—the fruits of men's fidelity to God and to his holy will (cf. Leo XIII, Encyclical Letter *Immortale Dei,* Nov. 1, 1885: *A.A.S.* 18 [1885], p. 161).

If, in view of peculiar circumstances obtaining among peoples, one religious body receives special legal recognition in the constitutional order of society, it is at the same time imperative that the right of all citizens and religious bodies to religious freedom should be recognized and made effective in practice.[15]

---

whole Church–State question. But more important, "civil authority" is more comprehensive; it includes all civil subordinate authorities and, it is hoped, eventual international authorities.

15 This paragraph is carefully worded. Cf. above, pp. 49-53. Several fathers, especially from "Catholic" countries, insisted that the document should explicitly affirm that "establishment" of a "religion of the State" is not *eo facto* condemned and that it is compatible with religious freedom. The first text (B) stated unconditionally that there is no incompatibility, but the reasons for the establishment are historical, not *a priori* theological. This affirmation was changed to the conditional: "If, in view. . . ."

Thus, the Council does not judge the intrinsic value of the "peculiar circumstances". Nor does it judge whether or not, ever or now, "peculiar circumstances" warrant establishment, or whether or not such establishment would always threaten full religious freedom for the minority or majority group.

Furthermore, if the reason for this paragraph was to pro-

Finally, since the equality of citizens before the law is an element of the common good of society, civil authority must see to it that this equality is never violated either openly or covertly for religious reasons, and that there is no discrimination among citizens on religious grounds.

From this it follows that it is wrong for a public authority to resort to force, intimidations or any other means to compel its citizens to profess or repudiate any religion or to hinder men from joining or leaving a religious community. All the more is it a violation of the will of God and of the sacred rights of the person and the family of nations when force is brought to bear in any way in order to wipe out a religion or repress it, whether in the whole of mankind or in any one region or in a particular community.[16]

---

vide for a possible established Roman Catholic Church, it recognizes the same privilege for any other established religious body, i.e., Protestant, Orthodox, Muslim, Buddhist, etc.

Finally, the "special legal recognition" does not mean that a State *must* be confessional when it grants some special recognition to a particular religious group.

An interestingly phrased promise from *The Church in the Modern World:* "The Church itself employs temporal things to the degree that its own proper mission demands. Nevertheless, it does not lodge its hope in privileges conferred by civil authority. Indeed, the Church stands ready to renounce the exercise of certain legitimately required rights if it becomes clear that their use raises doubt about the sincerity of its witness or that new conditions of life demand some other arrangement" (n. 76).

[16] The guilty are not named, but the reference is clearly to totalitarian regimes under Communist inspiration. *The Constitution on the Church* rejects that "unfortunate doctrine that attempts to build a society with no regard whatever for religion and destroys the religious freedom of its citizens" (n. 36).

The Limits of Religious Freedom

7. The right to religious freedom is exercised in human society; hence its exercise is subject to certain practical checks and controls.

Wherever there is use of any kind of freedom, the moral principle of personal and social responsibility is to be observed. In the exercise of their rights individual men and social groups are bound by the moral law to take into account the rights of others, their own duties toward others and the common welfare of all. Men are to deal with their fellows in justice and civility.

Furthermore, since society has the right to protect itself against possible abuses committed on the pretext of freedom of religion, it is the special duty of government to provide this protection. However, this must not be done in arbitrary fashion or by giving unfair advantage to one group. Its action is to be controlled by juridical norms which are in conformity with the objective moral order.[17] These norms arise out of the need for effective safeguard of the rights of all citizens and for peaceful settlement of conflicts of rights. They are needful too for an adequate care of that genuine public peace which comes about when men live together in good order [18] and in true justice,

---

[17] The laws restricting religious freedom must be morally just. There is no idolatry of the civil law independent from its moral justification.

[18] Archbishop Juan Aramburu (Tucumán, Argentina) was worried about the phrase "public peace" in (B) because it could be interpreted as an acceptance of the *status quo* and a forbidding of its disturbance. His example was "the movement for racial justice in the United States". He added: "The mere fact of being afraid to disrupt an existing social order can never be used as an excuse to prevent legitimate change

and for the proper guardianship of public morality. These things are basic to the common welfare;
they are what is meant by public order. For the
rest, the normal practice in society is the full range
of freedom: that is, man's freedom is to be respected as far as possible and is to be curtailed only
when and as far as necessary.[19]

---

in the interest of human betterment. The peace which may
not be disturbed is not any peace, but only that peace which
is in full accord with the moral order implanted by God in
human nature" (Council speech of Sept. 16, 1965).

[19] Nn. 6–7 carefully work out the very complicated theme:
the protection and fostering of the inalienable right to religious freedom, and the regulatory norms for governmental
limitation of the exercise of that right. To understand this
treatment, a distinction between the common good or welfare
of society and the public order is necessary.

The *common welfare* of society, as described in *Pacem in
terris* and repeated in the Declaration (n. 6), is "the sum
total of those conditions of social life which enable man to
achieve a fuller measure of perfection with some relative
ease". Chief among these conditions is the care or fostering of
human rights, and this includes the right to freedom in religious matters.

The *public order* of society, which is narrower in content
than common welfare, is constituted by those basic elements
of the common welfare which are so necessary that without
them true society cannot even exist. These essential elements
are: (1) the *political* good, or genuine public peace ("domestic tranquillity", says the U.S. Constitution) ; (2) the *moral*
good, which is public morality, at least its minimum standards;
(3) the *good of justice,* which is the secure juridical possession
and exercise of human and civil rights (cf. below, pp. 128-130).

With this distinction the Declaration treats the care of religious freedom and the limitation of its exercise.

All elements of society—individuals, groups, religious bodies,
governments—are charged with the common task of promoting
the common welfare, and thus with the positive care for the
maximum protection of all the rights, and the maximum performance of all the duties, of the human person. But each
should do this in a way proper to itself.

However, it is one thing for government to acknowledge
and protect the religious rights of its citizens and create condi-

Educating for the Exercise of Freedom

8. Modern man is subjected to many pressures. He runs the risk of losing the possibility of acting freely and responsibly. On the other hand, a considerable number seem inclined to use the name of freedom as the pretext for refusing to submit to any authority and for making light of the duty of obedience.

For this reason, this Vatican Council urges everyone, especially those responsible for the education of others, to do their utmost to form men who, on the one hand, will respect the moral order and be obedient to lawful authority, and who, on the other hand, will be lovers of freedom—in other words, men who will come to decisions on their own judgments and in the light of truth, govern their activities with a sense of responsibility and

---

tions that will help them in carrying out their religious duties (n. 6 and footnote 10). It is another thing for government to limit the exercise of these rights (n. 7). The norm for the first (*promotion*) is the *common welfare;* the norm for the second (*restriction*) is that fundamental part of the common welfare called *public order.* Thus, the *coercive* power of government is enlisted only when it needs to protect and vindicate those three basic elements of the common welfare: genuine public peace, public morality and the juridical possession and exercise of human and civil rights. The public exercise of one's right to religious freedom may not be inhibited unless a violation of public order has been proved. The legal norms are not arbitrary ones, but are to conform to the objective moral order.

Here, then, is the affirmation of "the free man under a limited government" (cf. below, p. 145). The freedom of man is to be respected as far as possible precisely as a perfection of the human person and thus as a positive contribution to the common welfare of society. The freedom of man is to be curtailed only when and as far as necessary, that is, only when and as far as it disturbs the public order.

strive for truth and justice in all things in willing cooperation with their fellowmen.

Religious freedom, therefore, ought to have this further purpose and aim: namely, that men may come to act with greater responsibility in fulfilling their duties in community life.

III

Religious Freedom in the Light of Revelation

The Roots of the Teaching on Religious Freedom in Revelation

9. The Declaration of this Vatican Council on the right of man to religious freedom is based on the dignity of the person. The requirements of this dignity have become more fully known to human reason through centuries of experience. What is more, this doctrine of freedom has its roots in divine revelation, and for this reason Christians are bound to respect it all the more conscientiously.

Although revelation does not explicitly affirm the right of man to immunity from external coercion in religious matters,[20] it does disclose the full

---

[20] Several criticisms were leveled against the treatment by (A) and (B) of "the doctrine of religious freedom in the light of revelation": "What are you trying to prove?" (C) introduced the explicit denial of "proving" immunity from coercion by means of revelation. But the Word of God does teach us much about the human person and his dignity (n. 9), the liberty of his act of faith (n. 10) and the full respect Christ and his disciples had for human freedom (n. 11).

For this second section, the Secretariat enlisted the help of biblical scholars: Frs. Barnabas M. Ahern, C.P., Yves Congar, O.P., Pierre Benoit, O.P., Stanislas Lyonnet, S.J., and Francis McCool, S.J.

dignity of the human person; it gives evidence of the respect which Christ showed toward the freedom with which man is to fulfill his duty of belief in the Word of God; it teaches us the spirit which disciples of such a master ought to make their own and to follow in every situation. These points shed further light upon the general principles on which the doctrine of this *Declaration on Religious Freedom* is based. The main point is that religious freedom in society is entirely consonant with the freedom of the act of Christian faith.

The Freedom of the Act of Faith

10. Man's response to God in faith must be free; therefore, no one is to be forced to embrace the Christian faith against his own will [21] (cf. *C.I.C.*, c. 1351; Pius XII, Allocution *To the Prelates, Auditors and Other Officials and Staff of the Tribunal of the Sacred Roman Rota*, Oct. 6, 1946: *A.A.S.* 38 [1946], p. 394; *idem*, Encyclical Letter *Mystici corporis*, June 29, 1943: *A.A.S.* 35 [1943], p. 243). This is one of the major tenets of Catholic teaching, one which is contained in the Word of God and constantly proclaimed by the Fathers of the Church.*

---

[21] "The Church severely forbids anyone to be forced to embrace the faith, or enticed to do so by unworthy means. At the same time, the Church strongly asserts the person's right not to be deterred from the faith by unjust hardship on the part of others" (*The Decree on the Church's Missionary Activity*, n. 13).

* Cf. Lactantius, *Divinarum Institutionum* V, 19: *C.S.E.L.* 19, pp. 463–465: *P.L.* 6, 614 and 616 (ch. 20); St. Ambrose, *Epistola ad Valentianum Imp.*, Ep. 21: *P.L.* 16, 1005; St. Augustine, *Contra litteras Petiliani* II, ch. 83: *C.S.E.L.* 52, p. 112: *P.L.* 43, 315; cf. C. 23, q. 5, c. 33 (ed. Friedberg, col. 939); *idem*, Ep. 23: *P.L.* 33, 98; *idem*, Ep. 34: *P.L.* 33, 132; *idem*, Ep. 35:

The act of faith is by its very nature a free act. Man has been redeemed by Christ the savior and through Christ Jesus called to be God's adopted son (cf. Eph. 1, 5). He cannot give his adherence to God revealing himself, unless the Father draws him (cf. Jn. 6, 44) to offer to God the reasonable and free submission of faith.[22] Therefore, the exclusion of any sort of coercion on the part of men in religious matters is completely in accord with the nature of faith. In consequence, the principle of religious freedom contributes greatly to the creation of an environment in which man can without hindrance be invited to Christian faith, embrace it of his own free will and give it practical expression in his life.

The Way of Acting of Christ and the Apostles

11. God calls man to serve him in spirit and in truth; hence he is bound in conscience but stands under no compulsion. God has regard for the dignity of the human person whom he himself

P.L. 33, 135; St. Gregory the Great, *Epistola ad Virgilium et Theodorum Episcopos Massiliae Galliarum*, Registrum Epistolarum I, 45: *M.G.H.*, Ep. 1, p. 72: *P.L.* 77, 510–511 (Book I, Ep. 47); *idem, Epistola ad Iohannem Episcopum Constantinopolitanum*, Registrum Epistolarum III, 52: *M.G.H.*, Ep. 1, p. 210: *P.L.* 77, 649 (Book III, Ep. 53); cf. D. 45, c. 1 (ed. Friedberg, col 160); Council of Toledo IV, c. 57: *Mansi* 10, 633; cf. D. 45, c. 5 (ed. Friedberg, cols. 161–162); Clement III, X., V, 6, 9 (ed. Friedberg, col. 774); Innocent III, *Epistola ad Arelatensem Archiepiscopum*, X., III, 42, 3 (ed Friedberg, col. 646).

22 "Though the same God is savior and creator, Lord of human history as well as salvation history, in the divine plan the rightful autonomy of the creature, and particularly of man, is not withdrawn. Rather he is reestablished in his own dignity and strengthened in it" (*The Church in the Modern World*, n. 41).

created; man is to be guided by his own judgment and he is to enjoy freedom.

This truth was given its highest demonstration in Christ Jesus, in whom God perfectly revealed himself and his ways with men. Christ is our master and our Lord (cf. Jn. 13, 13), and at the same time meek and humble of heart (cf. Mt. 11, 29). It was by patience that he invited and drew the disciples to himself (cf. Mt. 11, 28-30; Jn. 6, 67-68). He had indeed wrought miracles to illuminate his teaching and to establish its truth, but his intention was to rouse faith in his hearers and to confirm them in faith, not to exert coercion upon them (cf. Mt. 9, 28-29; Mk. 9, 23-24; 6, 5-6; Paul VI, Encyclical Letter *Ecclesiam suam,* Aug. 6, 1964: *A.A.S.* 56 [1964], pp. 642-643). He did indeed censure the unbelief of his listeners, but he left vengeance to God on the day of judgment (cf. Mt. 11, 20-24; Rom. 12, 19-20; 2 Thess. 1, 8). When he sent his apostles into the world, he said to them: "He who believes and is baptized will be saved; he who does not believe will be condemned" (Mk. 16, 16). He noted that weeds had been sown amid the wheat, but ordered both to be left growing until the harvest time at the end of the world (cf. Mt. 13, 30. 40-42). He refused to be a political messiah gaining mastery by force (cf. Mt. 4, 8-10; Jn. 6, 15), but preferred to call himself the Son of Man who came "to serve and to give his life as a ransom for the many" (Mk. 10, 45). He revealed himself as the perfect servant of God (cf. Is. 42, 1-4), who will not break the bruised reed or quench a smoldering wick" (Mt. 12, 20). He acknowledged the power of government and its rights when he ordered the paying of tribute to Caesar, but he gave clear warning that the higher rights of God are to be kept inviolate: "Render to Caesar the things that

are Caesar's and to God the things that are God's"
(Mt. 22, 21). In the end, when he completed
on the cross the work of redemption whereby he
achieved salvation and true freedom for men, he
brought his revelation to completion. He bore witness to the truth (cf. Jn. 18, 37), but he refused to
impose the truth by force on those who spoke
against it. Not by force of blows does his kingdom
assert its claims (cf. Mt. 26, 51-53; Jn. 18, 36); it
is established by witnessing to the truth and by
hearing the truth, and it extends its dominion by
the love whereby Christ, lifted up on the cross,
draws men to himself (cf. Jn. 12, 32).

Taught by the Word and example of Christ, the
apostles followed the same way. From the very
origins of the Church, the main tool of Christ's
disciples in their labors to convert men to faith in
Christ the Lord was the power of the Word of
God (cf. 1 Cor. 2, 3-5; 1 Thess. 2, 3-5), not coercion
or techniques unworthy of the Gospel. Steadfastly
they proclaimed to all the plan of God our savior
"who wills that all men should be saved and come
to the knowledge of the truth" (1 Tim. 2, 4). At the
same time, they showed respect for those of weaker
stuff, even if they were in error. In this way they demonstrated how "each one of us is to render to God an
account of himself" (Rom. 14, 12; cf. 14, 1-23; 1 Cor.
8, 9-13; 10, 23-33) and for that reason is bound to obey
his conscience. As with Christ himself, it was always
the aim of the apostles to bear witness to the truth
of God, showing no hesitation in "speaking the
Word with boldness" (Acts 4, 31) before people
and rulers alike (cf. Eph. 6, 19-20). They firmly
believed that the Gospel is indeed the power of
God for the salvation of all who have faith (cf.
Rom. 1, 16). Therefore, they rejected all "worldly
weapons" (cf. 2 Cor. 10, 4; 1 Thess. 5, 8-9) and

followed the example of Christ's gentleness and re-
spectfulness, preaching the Word of God with full
confidence that there was resident in this Word itself a divine power able to destroy all the forces
arrayed against God (cf. Eph. 6, 11-17) and bring
men to faith in Christ and to his service (cf. 2 Cor.
10, 3-5).

Like the master, so too the apostles recognized
legitimate civil authority. "For there is no power
except from God," the apostle teaches, and thereafter commands: "Let everyone be subject to the
governing authorities. . . . He who resists authority resists God's ordinance" (Rom. 13, 1-5; cf. 1
Pet. 2, 13-17). At the same time they were not afraid
to speak out against the public authorities when
they set themselves in opposition to God's holy
will: "It is necessary to obey God rather than
men" (Acts 5, 29; cf. Acts 4, 19-20). This is the
way along which the martyrs and other faithful
have walked through all ages and over all the
earth.

The Church in the Footsteps of Christ and the Apostles

12. In faithfulness to the truth of the Gospel,
the Church is following the way of Christ and the
apostles when it recognizes and supports the principles of religious freedom as befitting the dignity
of man and as being in accord with what God has
revealed. Over the ages the Church has pre-
served and handed on the teaching received from
the master and from the apostles. In the life of the
People of God as it has made its pilgrim way through
the vicissitudes of human history, there has at times
appeared a way of acting that was hardly in accord

with the spirit of the Gospel or even opposed to it.[23] Nevertheless, the doctrine of the Church has always stood firm: no one is to be coerced into faith.

The leaven of the Gospel has long been about its quiet work in the minds of men, and it has contributed greatly to a wider recognition, in the course of time, of the dignity of the human person, and to the conviction that in religious matters the person in society is to be kept free from any human coercion.

The Freedom of the Church

13. Of those things that concern the good of the Church and indeed the welfare of society here on earth—things, therefore, that are always and everywhere to be kept secure and defended against all injury—the most preeminent is that the Church should enjoy that full measure of freedom which its care for the salvation of men requires (cf. Leo XIII, Letter *Officio sanctissimo,* Dec. 22, 1887: *A.A.S.* 20 [1887], p. 269; *idem,* Letter *Ex litteris,* April 7, 1887: *A.A.S.* 19 [1886], p. 465). This is the sacred freedom with which the only-begotten Son endowed the Church which he purchased with his own blood. Indeed, this freedom belongs so intimately to the Church that to act against it is to act against the will of God. The freedom of the Church is the basic principle in the relations between the Church and public authorities and the whole civil order.

The Church is the spiritual authority estab-

---

23 Here, in strange understatement, the Council revealed once more the tension between the desire to express humble penitence for past faults (cf. *Decree on Ecumenism,* n. 8) and old reflexes of proud refusal to state the fact boldly.

lished by Christ the Lord with the duty, imposed by divine command, of going out into the world and preaching the Gospel to every creature (cf. Mk. 16, 15; Mt. 28, 18-20; Pius XII, Encyclical Letter *Summi pontificatus,* Oct. 20, 1939: *A.A.S.* 31 [1939], pp. 445-446). In this character the Church claims freedom for itself in human society and before every public authority. But the Church also claims freedom for itself in its character as a society of men who enjoy the right to live in civil society according to the tenets of the Christian faith (cf. Pius XI, Letter *Firmissimam constantiam,* March 28, 1937: *A.A.S.* 29 [1937], p. 196).

But it is not enough for the principle of religious freedom to receive verbal recognition or legal safeguards; it must be honestly implemented in practice. Only then does the Church possess by right and in practice stable conditions for the independence necessary in fulfilling its divine mission. This independence in society is precisely what the authorities of the Church have been insisting on with increasing urgency (cf. Pius XII, Allocution *Ci riesce,* Dec. 6, 1953: *A.A.S.* 45 [1953], p. 802). At the same time, the Christian faithful have the same civil right as other men to be free from interference in leading their lives according to their conscience. Therefore, a harmony exists between the freedom of the Church and that religious freedom which must be recognized as the right of all men and all communities and sanctioned by constitutional law.

The Task of the Church

14. In obedience to the divine commission to "make disciples of all nations" (Mt. 28, 19-20), the

Catholic Church must work with all urgency and concern "that the Word of God may speed on and triumph" (2 Thess. 3, 1).

The Church earnestly begs its children that "first of all, supplications, prayers, petitions, and acts of thanksgiving be made for all men. . . . For this is good and agreeable in the sight of God, our savior, who wills that all men be saved and come to the knowledge of the truth" (1 Tim. 2, 1-4).

In the formation of their consciences the Christian faithful ought carefully to attend to the holy and certain doctrine of the Church (cf. Pius XII, Radio Message of March 23, 1952: *A.A.S.* 44 [1952], pp. 270-278), for by the will of Christ the Church is the teacher of the truth. It is its duty to declare and teach authoritatively that truth which is Christ himself. It also is to use its authority to expound those principles of the moral order which have their origin in human nature itself. Furthermore, let Christians walk in wisdom in the face of those outside, "in the Holy Spirit, in unaffected love, in the Word of truth" (2 Cor. 6, 6-7), and let them do their utmost, even to the shedding of their blood, to spread the light of life with the confident courage of apostles (cf. Acts 4, 29).

The disciple has a grave obligation toward Christ, his master, to grow daily in the knowledge of the truth he has received from him, to be faithful in proclaiming it and active in defending it, never—be it understood—having recourse to means which go against the spirit of the Gospel. At the same time, the charity of Christ urges him to love and have prudence and patience in his dealings with those who are in error or in ignorance of the faith (cf. John XXIII, Encyclical Letter *Pacem in terris, op. cit.,* pp. 299-300). All is to be taken into account—the Christian duty to Christ, the life-giving Word which must be proclaimed, the rights of the human person and the measure of grace which God has given to each man in inviting him freely to accept and profess the faith.[24]

Conclusion

15. The fact is that modern man wants to be able to profess his religion freely in private and in public. Religious freedom has already been declared to be a civil right in most constitutions, and it is solemnly recognized in international docu-

---

[24] The firm profession of Roman Catholic ecclesiology now is clear. The "one true religion subsists in the Catholic and Apostolic Church" (n. 1), which is the Roman Catholic Church *(Constitution on the Church,* n. 8; cf. above, pp. 64-65, footnote 4).

True, like any other religious group, the Church claims freedom from coercive interference in its ministry and life because of the dignity of the human person which requires such freedom for men when they act in religious community (n. 4).

But the Church claims "for itself in human society and before every public authority" this immunity under a second title, and this is a *unique, privileged title*—the mandate given to the Church by Christ (n. 13). Precisely because it is the duty of the Church "to declare and teach authoritatively that truth which is Christ himself", it respects not only the truth to be preached but also the rights of the human person to whom it proclaims Christ, and "the measure of grace which God has given each man in inviting him freely to accept and profess the faith" (n. 14). Nevertheless, despite the Church's constant teaching that "no one is to be forced to embrace the Christian faith against his own will" (n. 10), the Church has not always shown that respect in practice (n. 12).

It should be mentioned that the Roman Catholic theologian should begin studying to what degree other Christian communities share in the *privileged* title to religious freedom, since other communions, in various ways, are Christian "means of salvation" *(media salutis)* which bear witness to Christ (cf. *Decree on Ecumenism,* nn. 3–4).

ments (cf. John XXIII, Encyclical Letter *Pacem in terris, op. cit.,* pp. 295-296).

There is another fact. Forms of government still exist under which, despite constitutional recognition of freedom of religious worship, the public authorities try to detach citizens from their religious allegiance and make life very difficult and dangerous for religious communities.

This Council gladly welcomes the first of these two facts as among the signs of the times. With sorrow, however, it denounces the other fact as only to be deplored. The Council exhorts Catholics —and it extends its plea to all men—to consider with great care how greatly necessary religious freedom is, especially in the present condition of the human family.

All nations are coming into even closer unity; men of different cultures and religions are being drawn together by closer bonds; there is a growing consciousness of the personal responsibility that every man has. All this is evident. But to establish and strengthen peaceful relationships and harmony in the whole of mankind, two further things are necessary: the constitutional guarantee of religious freedom, and respect for that highest of man's duties and rights—to conduct a religious life freely in society.

May the God and Father of all men grant that the human family may carefully observe religious freedom in society, and so be brought through the grace of Christ and the power of the Holy Spirit to that noble and everlasting "glorious freedom of the sons of God" (Rom. 8, 21).

*   *   *

The entire text and all the points which have been set forth in this Declaration have pleased the fathers of the sacred Council. And we, by the apostolic authority given us by Christ, together with the venerable fathers, approve, appoint and decree its contents in the Holy Spirit and order that what has been decided in the Council be promulgated to the glory of God.

Rome, in St. Peter's Basilica, December 7, 1965

Paul, Bishop of the Catholic Church
(The signatures of the fathers follow)

APPENDIX I

Bishop de Smedt's Report on Religious Liberty *

Very many conciliar fathers have insistently demanded that this sacred Synod clearly explain and proclaim the right of man to religious liberty. Among the reasons given, four principal ones should be listed:

1. *Truth:* The Church must teach and defend the right to religious liberty because there is a question of the truth, care of which was committed to it by Christ;

2. *Defense:* The Church cannot remain silent today when almost half of mankind is deprived of religious liberty by atheistic materialism of various kinds;

3. *Peaceful Social Life:* Today in all nations of the world, men who adhere to different religions or who lack all religious belief must live together in one and the same human society; in the light of truth, the Church should point the way toward living together peacefully;

4. *Ecumenism:* Many non-Catholics harbor an aversion against the Church or at least suspect

---

* The text of this speech is taken from *Council Speeches of Vatican II*, eds. Hans Kung, Yves Congar, O.P., and Daniel O'Hanlon, S.J. (Glen Rock, New Jersey: Paulist Press [1964], pp. 237-253).

it of a kind of Machiavellism because we seem to them to demand the free exercise of religion when Catholics are in a minority in any nation and at the same time refuse and deny the same religious liberty when Catholics are in the majority.

Religious liberty is such a grave problem in modern society that it cannot be omitted in a pastoral decree on ecumenism. Therefore, we submit to your deliberations this fifth chapter of our schema on ecumenism. The Secretariat for Promoting Christian Unity, to the best of its ability, has carefully watched over the preparation of this material.

Since we are treating of a most difficult question and at the same time one of great importance in modern life, the authors of the schema cherish the hope that your attention and pastoral consideration will emend what needs emendation and perfect what is still imperfect in the schema now offered to you.

The term "religious liberty" has a definite meaning in our text. In the forthcoming discussion, great confusion might arise if any of the fathers give to the expression a meaning that differs from the one intended by the text.

When religious liberty is defended, it is not asserted that it is proper for man to consider the religious problem according to his own whim without any moral obligation and decide for himself according to his own will whether or not to embrace religion (religious indifferentism).

Nor is it affirmed that the human conscience is free in the sense that it is, as it were, outside of the law, absolved from any obligation toward God (laicism).

Nor is it said that falsehood is to be considered on an equal footing with truth, as though there were no objective norm of truth (doctrinal relativism).

Nor is it admitted that man in any way has a quasi right to maintain a peaceful complacency in the midst of uncertainty (dilettantistic pessimism).

If anyone were to insist upon giving any of the aforesaid meanings to "religious liberty" he would attribute to our text a meaning which neither the words nor our intention possesses.

What therefore is meant in the text by "religious liberty"? Positively, religious liberty is the right of the human person to the free exercise of religion according to the dictates of his conscience. Negatively, it is immunity from all external force in his personal relations with God, which the conscience of man vindicates to itself.

Religious liberty implies human autonomy, not from within, certainly, but from without. From within, man is not freed of the obligations toward the religious problem. From without, his liberty is offended when obedience to the dictates of his conscience in religious matters is impeded.

At this point two questions must be asked: (1) Can each man claim for himself religious liberty as a sacred right given to him by God? (2) Is there —and to what extent—a duty on the part of others to recognize the aforesaid religious liberty?

Our Decree, since it is pastoral, tries to treat the present matter especially from the practical point of view and, after the manner of John XXIII, will carefully strive to remove the whole question from that world of abstractions which was so dear to the nineteenth century. The question is therefore put regarding real man in his real dealings with other men, in contemporary human and civil societies.

I

The first pastoral problem which must be examined now by this sacred synod is this: *How must Catholics, because of their faith, conduct themselves toward men who do not belong to the Catholic faith?* We propose the following answer for your deliberations:

1. All Catholics are invited by Christ to strive by prayer, penance, witness and evangelizing in the Holy Spirit to bring our non-Catholic brothers to the blessing of the evangelical light and of the life of the Church. The sacred, absolute right of God, as well as the evangelical and natural truths, must always and everywhere be honored and observed by them.

2. They must abstain from all direct coercion. Although God wills all men to be saved and to come to the knowledge of the truth, the disciples of Christ may not infringe upon the religious liberty of the individual person. On the contrary, they must respect and esteem the right and duty of non-Catholics to follow the dictate of their own conscience, even when, after sincere and sufficient study, it errs in good faith.

What is the reason of faith why non-Catholics can be forced by no one to admit the Catholic doctrine against their conscience? This reason is to be found in the very nature of the act of faith. For this act, on God's part, is a supernatural gift which the Holy Spirit most freely gives to whom and when he wills; and, on man's part, it is and must be an assent which man freely gives to God.

3. All Catholics are bound, by the command of the Lord, to love and to help their non-Catholic brothers with a sincere and active charity.

II

At this point, the schema takes a step forward and asserts that each and every man who follows his conscience in religious matters has a natural right to true and authentic religious liberty for the whole human family, for all religious groups, for each human person whether his conscience be sincere (*rectam*) and true, or sincere and false concerning faith, provided only that he sincerely follow the dictate of conscience. Therefore, a general principle is laid down: *no human person can be the object of coercion or intolerance.*

What is the reason why observance of religious liberty is demanded of all? The human person endowed with conscious and free activity, since he can fulfill the will of God only as the divine law is perceived through the dictate of conscience, can obtain his ultimate end only by prudently forming the judgment of conscience and by faithfully carrying out its dictate.

From the nature of things, in forming this judgment whereby man tries freely to conform to the absolute demands of God's rights, neither any other man nor any human institution can take the place of free judgment of man's conscience. Therefore, the man who sincerely obeys his own conscience intends to obey God himself, although at times confusedly and unknowingly, and is to be considered worthy of esteem.

When religious liberty is violated, then the very freedom of the human person is violated in its principal matter, in a fundamental demand, in man's ordination to the supreme and ultimate end. The greatest injury is to prevent a man from worshiping God and obeying God according to the dictate of his own conscience.

III

The schema takes still another step forward and enters upon a most difficult question. Religious liberty would be fruitless and empty if men were not able to carry out the dictate of their conscience in external acts whether in private life, in social life or in public life, or if human persons were prevented from forming religious groups whose members could worship the supreme deity by common and social acts and lead a religious life.

Here, however, there arises a most difficult problem, for if a human person carries out the dictates of his conscience by external acts, there is a danger of violating the rights and duties of another or of others. Since man is a social being and since in the human family men are subject to error and to sin, the conflict of rights and the conflict of duties cannot always be avoided. From this it is evident *the right and duty to manifest externally the dictate of conscience is not unlimited, but can be—at times must be—tempered and regulated for the common good.*

This ordering of the common good must be done juridically in human society and belongs to public authority (*potestati publicae*). "One of the fundamental duties of civil authorities, therefore," we read in *Pacem in terris,* n. 62, "is to coordinate social relations in such fashion that the exercise of one man's rights does not threaten others in the exercise of their own rights nor hinder them in the fulfillment of their duties. Finally, the rights of all should be effectively safeguarded and, if they have been violated, completely restored."

How is public authority to carry out this duty? In establishing order for the common good, public authority can never act contrary to the order of justice established by God. As St. Thomas says: "Human law is truly law to the extent that it is in accordance with right reason, and therefore it is evident that it is derived from the eternal law. Insofar as it departs from reason, it is a so-called 'wicked law', and therefore is not truly a law but a kind of violence" (I-II, q. 93, a. 3, ad 2).

Recent Roman pontiffs again and again have bewailed the fact that not a few governments have gone too far in this matter, ignoring and violating religious liberty. In our own day there are some regions in which tolerance in religious matters has been so little observed that the supreme pontiff, Paul VI, in his allocution to the fathers of the Vatican Council II on September 29, 1963, said, speaking of violated right to religious liberty: "Because of sufferings of this kind, with what sadness we are affected, and how deeply we are grieved, when we behold that in some territories religious liberty, together with other principal rights of man, is suppressed by the principles and acts of those who do not tolerate opinions different from theirs on politics, on races of men or on religion of any kind. We are sorrowed also by many injuries which are done to those who would like to profess their religion honestly and freely."

IV

In order that we might clearly understand the doctrine of the Church on the extent and limits of the civil power's duty relating to religious liberty, we must, in a few words, develop the history of this doctrine. Bear with me, Venerable Fathers, if I seem to make more than just demands on your patience. But the Secretariat for Promoting Christian Unity is convinced that many difficulties and confusions can be avoided in this study of the schema if, before the discussion begins, I show very briefly what the supreme pontiffs since the time of Pius IX have taught concerning the duties of public authority in religious matters.

On the question of religious liberty, the principal document is the encyclical *Pacem in terris* in which Pope John XXIII especially developed these two points of doctrine: (1) By the law of nature, the human person has the right to the free exercise of religion in society according to the dictates of a sincere conscience (*conscientia recta*), whether the conscience be true (*conscientia vera*) or the captive either of error or of inadequate knowledge of truth and of sacred things. (2) To this right corresponds the duty incumbent upon other men and the public authority to recognize and respect that right in such a way that the human person in society is kept immune from all coercion of any kind (cf. *A.A.S.* 55 [1963], p. 299; also cf. pp. 264 and 273-274).

Moreover, this doctrine must be understood as the contemporary terminus of a process of evolution both in the doctrine on the dignity of the human person and in the Church's pastoral solicitude for man's freedom. This doctrinal evolution took place according to a twofold law:

1. *Law of continuity:* The Church's doctrine and solicitude are always self-consistent, always remain the same. This perennial doctrine can be expressed in the words of Pope John: "The dignity of the human person demands this, that in his actions man should enjoy his own counsel and freedom" (*ibid.,* p. 265). This doctrine has its deepest roots in the sacred scriptures which teach that man was made to the image of God. From this

doctrine stems the continual pastoral solicitude of the Church for man's true freedom.

2. *Law of progress:* The ecclesiastical magisterium adapts, explains and defends genuine doctrine according to the demands of errors which are spread and according to the needs which arise from the development of man and of society. By this progress, the mind of the Church is led to search more deeply into doctrine and to understand it more clearly.

In this way, there has arisen in two areas a distinction which no one has explained more clearly than Pope John XXIII in his encyclical *Pacem in terris:* (1) A clearer distinction between false *philosophical teachings* and the *endeavors and institutions* which these ideologies give rise to or nourish. While on the one hand the ideologies are always to be condemned, on the other hand the economic, social and civil institutions which have arisen therefrom can contain something that is good and worthy of approval. (2) A clearer distinction between *errors* and the *person* who errs in good faith. While on the one hand errors must always be rejected, on the other hand the man in error "does not cease to be endowed with human nature, nor does he ever lose his dignity as a person, due consideration of which must always be maintained" (*ibid.,* pp. 299-300).

These two laws of continuity and progress must be kept before our eyes always when the documents of the Apostolic See are read and interpreted.

V

In this way the door is opened to a correct understanding of many pontifical documents which in the nineteenth century treated of religious liberty in such words that this liberty appeared as something that had to be condemned. The clearest example is found in the encyclical *Quanta cura* of Pius IX, in which we read: "From this completely false concept of social rule [naturalism], they do not hesitate to foster that erroneous opinion which is especially injurious to the Catholic Church and the salvation of souls, called by our predecessor Gregory XVI *deliramentum,* namely, that freedom of conscience and of cults is the proper right of each man and this should be proclaimed and asserted in every rightly constituted society" (*A.S.S.* 3 [1867], p. 162).

As is evident, this freedom of conscience is condemned because of the ideology of the rationalists who founded their conclusions upon the principle that the individual conscience is under no law, and therefore, is subject to no divinely given norms (cf. *Syllabus,* prop. 3: *A.S.S.* 3, p. 168). Freedom of worship is condemned also when it is based upon religious indifferentism (*ibid.,* prop. 15, p. 170). Finally there is condemned that separation of the Church from the State which is based upon the rationalistic principle of the juridical omnicompetence of the State, according to which the Church is to be incorporated into the monistic organism of the State and is to be subjected to its supreme authority (*ibid.,* prop. 39, p. 172).

To understand those condemnations correctly, we must see in them the constant doctrine and solicitude of the Church concerning the true dignity of the human person and his true liberty (law of continuity). For the ultimate basis of human dignity lies in the fact that man is a creature of God. He is not God himself, but an image of God. From this absolute dependence of man upon God there flows every right and duty of man to claim for himself and for others true religious liberty. For man is subjectively bound to worship God according to the sincere dictates of his own conscience (*juxta rectam suae conscientiae normam*) because objectively he is absolutely dependent upon God.

In order, therefore, that his absolute dependence upon God might not be infringed in any way, man must not be impeded in any way by others or even by public authority from freely practicing his religion. Therefore, in opposing the philosophical and political tenets of laicism, the Church was fighting for the dignity and true liberty of the human person. In accordance with the law of continuity, then, the Church, in spite of changing conditions, has remained consistent both in the past and in the present.

Leo XIII had already started this doctrinal development when he distinguished clearly between the Church, the People of God, and the civil society, a terrestrial and temporal people (cf. *Immortale Dei: A.S.S.* 18 [1885], pp. 166-167). By this means he opened the way to a new affirmation of the due and lawful autonomy which belongs to the civil order and to its juridical dispositions. Because of this, it was possible to take a step forward (law of progress) toward a new judgment on "modern freedoms".

These freedoms can be tolerated (cf. *ibid.*, p. 174; *Libertas praestantissimum: A.S.S.* 20 [1887], pp. 609-610). And yet they were only to be *tolerated*. The reason was evident. For at that time in Europe the regimes which proclaimed the modern freedoms, religious liberty among them, consciously drew their inspiration from the laicist ideology. There was danger, therefore—Leo XIII sensed this—that the civil and political institutions of this kind of republic, since they were of laicist orientation, would lead to such abuses that they would necessarily do violence to the dignity and true liberty of the human person. In accordance with the law of continuity, what was dear to Leo XIII is always dear to the Church—the safeguarding of the human person.

With the rise of State totalitarianism in its various forms, Pope Pius XI brought pastoral and doctrinal development to a new height. There is no longer any danger, as there was in the nineteenth century, that the false concept of liberty might do violence to human dignity. There is a new danger that every kind of human and civil liberty, and above all religious liberty, will be destroyed. For this reason, the Church is beginning in a new way to manifest its concern, which through the centuries has never wavered, for human liberty and dignity. With the increase of its pastoral concern, the Church's doctrine continues to develop.

Faithfully observing the law of continuity, Pius XI maintained the unstinting opposition of the Church to anti-religious laicism: "Those things which Pius X condemned we also condemn; as often as there is in 'laicism' any meaning or purpose that is harmful or contrary to God or religion, we condemn laicism, and openly declare that it must be condemned, as alien to God and religion" (*Maximam gravissimamque: A.A.S.* 16 [1924], p. 10).

But observing the rule of progress no less, Pius XI introduced a new distinction which was of great importance for a deeper understanding of Catholic doctrine. He made a distinction between the "freedom of conscience" and the "freedom of consciences". The former he rejected as "equivocal", as often used by the laicist to signify "an absolute independence of conscience, which is an absurdity in man who was created and redeemed by God"; the latter, however—"freedom of consciences"— he accepted, stating that he would joyfully fight the good fight for "freedom of consciences" (*Non abbiamo bisogno: A.A.S.* 23 [1931], pp. 301-302) .

Moreover, Pius XI not only fought for the religious liberty of the faithful, but he was at the same time compelled to show pastoral concern on a wider basis. For not only the Christian, but human reality was at stake, if we can rightly distinguish between two things that are in reality one.

By way of new advances, Pius XI developed a truly liberal and Christian doctrine when he taught: "Man as a person possesses God-given rights which must remain immune from all denial, privation or interference on the part of society" (*Mit brennender Sorge: A.A.S.* 29 [1937], p. 159). And he continues in no ambiguous words: "The believer possesses the inalienable right to profess his faith and to practice it in a proper way. Laws which interfere with or render difficult this profession and practice are in contradiction to the natural law" (*ibid.*, p. 160) . No one who understands the condition of the times and the purpose of this encyclical can fail to understand the universal intent of this statement.

Deeply sharing the pastoral solicitude of his predecessor, Pius XII developed further and expanded his doctrine (law of progress) . One thing he kept before his mind: the human person, created by God, redeemed by Christ Jesus, yet placed in stringent circumstances and surrounded on all sides by dangers.

In this context of doctrine and pastoral solicitude (law of continuity) we must read the text which in this matter is supreme. Enumerating "the fundamental rights of the person" which must be recognized and respected in every well ordered society, he repeats the doctrine of Pius XI and vests it with new authority, affirming "the right to the private and public worship of God, including *'actio caritativa'* " (Radio Message of Dec. 24, 1942: *A.A.S.* 35 [1943], p. 19).

The Roman pontiff did not propose this doctrine as a tenuous opinion or as a theory belonging to the schools. On the contrary, he carries the doctrine to its juridicial conclusions so that it becomes a principle according to which just limits are placed on public authority: "The chief duty of any public authority is to safeguard the inviolable rights that are proper to men and so to provide that each one might more easily fulfill his duties" (Radio Message of June 1, 1941: *A.A.S.* 33 [1941], p. 200).

Here we must recall especially the doctrine of Pius XII on the limitation of the State because it deals with the suppression of errors within society: "Could it be that in certain circumstances he [God] would not give men any mandate, would not impose any duty, and would not even communicate the right to impede or to repress what is erroneous and false? A look at things as they are gives an affirmative answer." Then having cited the example of divine providence, he proceeds: "Hence the affirmation: religious and moral error must always be impeded when it is possible because toleration of them is in itself immoral, is not valid absolutely and unconditionally. Moreover, God has not given even to human authority such an absolute and universal command in matters of faith and morality. Such a command is unknown to the common convictions of mankind, to Christian conscience, to the sources of revelation and to the practice of the Church" (Allocation *Ci riesce: A.A.S.* 45 [1953], pp. 798-799).

This declaration (law of progress) is of the greatest importance for our question, especially if we keep in mind what was in the past held concerning the role of the State.

At the end of this historical development comes the encyclical *Pacem in terris.* This document comes forth as a ripe fruit of a slow process of growth which has taken place within the Church, under the light of the Holy Spirit, throughout the whole of the last century.

Our schema had already been prepared and had been studied by the Central Commission and by the Commission for Coordination when Pope John, on April 11 of this year, published his last encyclical, *Pacem in terris.* We believe that our text is in complete conformity with his pellucid doctrine which was received within the Church and outside the Church with unprecedented praise.

We now submit for your consideration this text. In the historical conspectus of this doctrine, we have shown that in the pontifical documents, along with continuity, we must look for a progressive spelling-out of doctrine. It is evident that certain quotations from the popes, because of a difference in words, can be put in opposition to our schema. But I beseech you, Venerable Fathers, not to force the text to speak outside of its historical and doctrinal context—not, in other words, to make the fish swim out of water.

Let our document be studied as it stands. It is not a dogmatic treatise, but a pastoral Decree directed to men of our time. The whole world is waiting for this Decree. The voice of the Church on religious liberty is being waited for in universities, in national and international organizations, in Christian and non-Christian communities, in the newspapers and in public opinion—and it is being waited for with urgent expectancy.

We hope that it will be possible to complete the discussion and the approbation of this very brief but very important Decree before the end of this second session. How fruitful our work would appear to the world if the conciliar fathers, with the voice of Peter's successor, could announce this liberating doctrine on religious liberty!

Venerable Fathers, we will add our labors to yours. Our Secretariat will study your emendations most attentively and also with the utmost speed. We will work day and night. But our hope is in the Lord. May Jesus Christ assist all of us with his grace. If at the end of this session he asks of us: "Young men, do you have any fish?", seeing the faith and goodwill of this Council, he might say to their successors what once he said to the apostles: "Cast the net to the right of the boat, and you will find" (Jn. 21, 6).

APPENDIX II

NOTE: *In June, 1965, along with the revised text of the Declaration, the Secretariat for Promoting Christian Unity sent to the Council fathers a twenty-five page Report (relatio) in two parts.*

The first part outlined those positive and negative criticisms of the November, 1964 text which the fathers had submitted in writing to the Secretariat after the third session.

The second part outlined the method and principles used in the redrafting. This method and these principles were the basis for all future revisions. Thus, this second part, slightly adapted, is here presented.

T.F.S.

The Method and Principles of the Declaration

I. THE MEANING OF FREEDOM

"Religious freedom" today is a technical term, and the Declaration accurately describes its meaning. However, the document also uses the word "libertas" in other senses which will easily be detected according to the context:

1. *Physical freedom:* freedom of choice, or the faculty of self-determination in acting.

2. *Psychological:* the consciousness of one's free will, of the ability to act on one's own responsibility, and one's dignity as a consequence of freedom.

3. *Moral:* (a) understood *positively:* the faculty of self-determination in fulfilling the moral law in all its fullness, and therefore also in regard to matters pertaining to man's relation to God. In this sense, the more completely men fulfill the moral law and morally perfect themselves, the more free they become; (b) understood *negatively:* the ability to set aside the moral law freely. In this sense, the more freely men reject or violate the moral law, the more they diminish their own genuine freedom, as scripture says: "Everyone who commits sin is a slave of sin" (Jn. 8, 34). This freedom is also called *physical* freedom. In this sense, men endowed with free will are physically able to reject the moral law, but they are morally bound to fulfill it.

4. *Evangelical:* the freedom with which men, by the truth of the Gospel and the grace of the Holy Spirit, are made free from sin and from the devil and live in holy friendship with God through Christ in the Spirit, until they finally attain perfect freedom in glory.

5. *Ecclesiastical:* the freedom to which the Church is entitled, by Christ's command, in carrying out its mission.

6. *Religious:* the immunity from force on the part of individuals, social groups and any human power, as set forth in the Declaration.

This last freedom, religious freedom, is quite distinct from all the other freedoms, although it is nevertheless intimately connected with them. This is true, first of all, because it has its basis in those freedoms, although in different ways:

1. In physical freedom: If man were not endowed with freedom of choice, there could be no discussion about his religious freedom or about any of the other freedoms.

2. In psychological freedom: Because this freedom implies man's responsibility for his actions, it also implies the dignity of the person in the ontological order, especially as that dignity is understood today.

3. In moral freedom: Out of man's duty to offer worship to God according to the dictate of his conscience, there arises in him a freedom with regard to other men—a right to immunity from coercion. More briefly, out of this freedom as a duty toward God there arises in man a freedom with regard to other men.

4. In evangelical freedom: Men are raised by Christ the redeemer to the dignity of the sons of God so that in their relations with God the Father liberty may be lived, especially as charity: "Rather are we to practice the truth in love, and so grow up in all things in him who is the head, Christ" (Eph. 4, 15). Furthermore, according to the Lord's command, the things that are to be rendered to God are clearly distinguished from those that are due to Caesar. As history shows, men who became Christians more and more insistently claimed liberty for themselves as the right to immunity from force, especially coercion by civil powers.

5. In ecclesiastical freedom: The Church, fulfilling its mission in the course of time in the entire human family, has helped, and continues to help men to understand more deeply their own genuine dignity as persons ordered to a supernatural end. That end is God himself. Eventually he is to be possessed completely in eternal glory. Sec-

ondly, the Church, unceasingly defending the liberty which it has by Christ's commandment, likewise has helped and still helps to bring it about that civil authority, in the exercise of its duties, does not pass beyond the limits of its proper competence. These things constitute the unshakable foundation for religious freedom, that is, the right to immunity from force in matters of religion.

On other grounds, too, religious freedom is connected with the other freedoms. For, by its nature, it aims at this, and therefore needs to be regulated, that the other freedoms—especially moral, evangelical and ecclesiastical freedom—may be the more easily and more fully exercised. In fact, where religious freedom is recognized, encouraged and effectively protected, rather than placing obstacles in the way, it provides incentives and offers helps, so that all men may be able to fulfill their religious duties according to the dictate of their own consciences, and so that the Church, too, may freely carry out its mission.

From all this we conclude that religious freedom, while on the one hand based on all the other freedoms and required by them, is on the other hand ordered toward this, that freedom, both as a duty and as a charity to fellowmen, may be exercised with greater ease and fullness.

II. Method Followed in the Declaration

The Declaration begins with the statement of fact that today religious freedom is taken to be a technical juridical concept admitted in very many civil constitutions.

The relations between the people and their

governments, as well as relations among the people themselves, are subject to rules and regulations. This concept was the result of a rather long historical, political and moral development, but it was not until the 18th century that it began to have force and effect. The question of religious freedom, therefore, pertains to the civil order. Thus, it must be kept distinct from other questions that pertain to theology: the meaning and scope of that evangelical liberty with which Christ has made us free (cf. Gal. 5, 1) and the relation between freedom and authority within the Church itself.

The Declaration draws its first argument for religious freedom from reason (nn. 3-8). In formulating this argument, it appeals to modern man's increased awareness of the dignity of the person, and to the demand for civil liberty that is the consequence of that awareness. One must note, however, that this argument is not based on the mere fact of this increased awareness, or on the mere fact of the demand for civil liberty, as though the Church were yielding to public opinion or indulging in a sort of juridical positivism. Far from it. On the contrary, the argument is really based upon the truth of personal dignity which the present-day consciousness makes manifest, and consequently upon justice itself which demands that freedom due to a person.

Then, in nn. 9-13, the Declaration considers religious freedom in the light of revelation. The purpose of this section is not to prove either exegetically or theologically that man's right to religious freedom is a valid right. That would be foolish and indeed impossible. The purpose of this consideration is rather to explain and show clearly how the modern technical and juridical concept has its roots in the written Word of God, and how it is consistent and in harmony with pertinent revealed truths, that is to say, with scriptural doctrine about the freedom of the act of faith and about the liberty that is proper to the Church.

A different method was also proposed. Its proponents say that the scriptural and theological doctrine about man's freedom should be explained first, and only then should one pass on to the argument from reason. It is more fitting, they maintain, for an Ecumenical Council to speak out of the treasury of Catholic doctrine and in conciliar language and style. It should not offer arguments, but rather proclaim the truth: in this case, the truth about man's freedom, which is much more profoundly rooted in sacred scripture.

But the Secretariat for Promoting Christian Unity could not entirely agree with the reasons of these Council fathers. The Declaration deals with a particular question. It does not explicitly treat man's freedom in general. The question should not be confused with others, however closely connected with them it may be. Furthermore, in declaring its mind on the matter of religious freedom, Vatican Council II wishes to be heard, and to be heard favorably, by all men throughout the world, and not only by Catholics. Very many well understand that this question about religious freedom is formally a juridical, political and ethical question, and it must therefore be resolved by rational arguments confirmed by experience in the secular world.

It is evident and readily granted that scriptural teaching about the dignity of man and about the freedom bestowed upon him by grace is indeed more profound than that doctrine as acquired by natural reason. Certainly it should be explained more and more widely to the faithful how, according to the Apostle, they have been called to freedom. But between that scriptural doctrine and the modern concept of religious freedom in human society there is a vast distance. Civil liberty, to be sure, is in a certain sense required by evangelical freedom, but just how it is required is a matter of dispute among experts. However, one thing is certain. Religious freedom cannot be logically deduced, so to speak, from evangelical freedom, as though the former were a juridical consequence of the latter. For the connection between these two freedoms is more easily perceived, it would seem, by an examination of historical experience, rather than by mere logical argumentation. This is suggested in the Declaration itself, where reference is made to the leaven of the Gospel quietly and fruitfully working among men through the ages (n. 12).

III. Reason for the Doctrine in the Declaration

1. *Connection with the Teaching on Society.* The teaching has its proper organic setting in the general doctrine about the proper ordering of human society, as this doctrine has been developed by supreme pontiffs of our time, especially by Pius XII and John XXIII. The four supreme principles of such regulation are thus summed up: "The order which prevails in human society is of an immaterial nature. Grounded as it is in *truth,* it must function according to the norms of *justice,* it should be inspired and perfected *by mutual love,* and finally it should be brought to an ever more refined and human balance *in freedom*" (*Pacem in Terris,* April

11, 1963: *A.A.S.* 55 [1963], p. 266). According to these principles, which derive their origin from God who is the First Truth, human society must be regulated in order to be rightly established and fruitful and suited to the dignity of men (*ibid.,* p. 267).

2. *Primary Truth.* Human society is grounded entirely on the truth about the human person and his dignity, as on a truly fundamental truth. It is from this that society derives all its aspirations for justice, for charity and for complete freedom. Pope Pius XII placed this truth firmly in its fundamental place. Pope John XXIII followed in the same path: "Any human society, if it is to be well ordered and beneficial, must lay down as a foundation this principle: that every human being is a person, that is, he has a nature endowed with intelligence and free will. Indeed, precisely because he is a person, he has rights and obligations flowing directly and simultaneously from his very nature. And as these rights and obligations are universal and inviolable, they cannot in any way be surrendered" (*ibid.,* p. 259).

3. *Notion of Personal Dignity.* The dignity of the human person demands above all "that one should act on his own decision, of set purpose and from a consciousness of his obligation, without being moved by force or pressure brought to bear upon him for the most part from without" (*ibid.,* p. 265). On this point St. Thomas says: "[St. Paul] indicates their [the Gentiles'] dignity in this: having no law, they are a law unto themselves, inasmuch as they perform for themselves the function of a law, instructing and inducing themselves toward what is good," because, as the Philosopher says in his *Ethics* (ch. XI), law is a pronouncement imposing constraint, emanating from prudence and reason. And therefore, as we read in 1 Tim. 1, 9,

the law is not made for the just—that is to say, the just man is not compelled by an external law—but *the law was made for the unjust* who need to be compelled by an external agent. And this is the highest degree of dignity in men, that they are induced to do good not by others, but by themselves. The second degree of dignity is found in those who are induced by another but not by the use of force. The third degree is had in those who do need force in order to become good men. The fourth degree belongs to those who cannot be directed toward the good even by force as in Jer. 2, 30: "In vain have I struck your children; they have not received correction" (*Com. in Eph. ad Rom.*, c. 2, lect. 3).

The dignity of the human person stands out most clearly from those divinely revealed truths by which we are taught that man was created in the image of God, redeemed by the blood of Christ, and by heavenly grace made a son of God and heir to his eternal glory. The purpose of this was that man, by cooperating with divine grace, might be able to move himself freely toward his highest good, which is God himself. But this essential dignity of the human person is also a truth discoverable by human reason. In fact, it is a truth long ago made known to man. But in our time men have become more and more conscious of this truth, and, what is more important, they have more fully perceived the demands it makes upon them as regards the establishing and regulating of social structures. They are demanding their civil liberties in order that in society they may live a life worthy of a human being. These yearnings of the human spirit for freedom are the natural consequence of understanding the truth, and on that truth about the human person are based the rights that men are demanding.

4. *Notion of a Free Society.* To this truth about human dignity corresponds the concept of a free society. A free society is that in which reponsible freedom is conceived as something that is first of all due to men from justice, and, at the same time, something that is to be loved by all men as a good that is most pertinent to their common good.

5. *Duty of the Government.* Since the common good consists primarily in the proper observance of the rights and duties of the human person, truth demands that "the chief concern of civil authorities must therefore be to ensure, on the one hand, that these rights be acknowledge, respected, co-ordinated with other rights, defended and promoted, and, on the other hand, that every man be able more easily to carry out his own duties. For to safeguard the inviolable rights of the human person, and to facilitate the fulfillment of his duties, is the paramount duty of every public authority" *(Pacem in terris, op. cit.,* p. 274) .

6. *Norm of Law.* Likewise based on this truth of human dignity is the traditional norm of law, according to which man must be allowed as much freedom as possible, and only as much restriction imposed upon him as is necessary. In other words, the use of freedom must not be restricted, except for a valid, proportionate and necessitating reason.

Man, crippled as he is by the effects of original sin, too often abuses his freedom, makes mistakes and commits many evils. On the other hand, there is no absolute moral principle requiring that all evils must be impeded so far as possible. Not even God himself has given to any human authority that kind of absolute and universal mandate (cf. Pius XII, Allocution *Ci riesce,* Dec. 6, 1953: *A.A.S.* 45 [1953], p. 799). On the contrary, there is a presumption of law in favor of a person's freedom or for his immunity from any coercion that would impede him from acting according to his own judgment. But this presumption yields only to a fact, namely, the necessity for such restriction, and that necessity must be proved in each particular case. In other words, a person's right to freedom must prevail unless in the given instance the right of others to restrict the use of freedom can be proved by valid reasons.

7. *Religious Freedom.* All these above principles are especially valid in what pertains to the goods of the human spirit; for example, the search for truth and the publishing of one's own opinion, the cultivation of the sciences and arts, etc. These principles must be observed even more carefully in regard to matters pertaining to religion. For religion, or man's relation and duty toward God, is a personal and most private good of the individual, above all his other goods. Moreover, a religious matter is by its nature such that, in principle, every kind of force is alien to it. In religious matters, therefore, a certain zone of freedom, so to speak, must be observed, and the greatest care taken, lest the bounds of religious freedom be circumscribed without evident necessity.

To be more specific, it is on the truth of the dignity of the human person, and on the true principles for the right ordering of society as derived from a consideration of personal dignity, that man's right to freedom, or to immunity from force in matters of religion, is really based. And this immunity is twofold: no one ought to be compelled to act against his conscience, and no one must be prevented from acting in accordance with his conscience. Each of these immunities is a strict right. The former is absolutely inviolable, but the latter can cease to be valid in a particular case, that is, if the necessity of a restriction of liberty by legitimate authority is duly proved.

But such necessity of restricting freedom in matters of religion arises only when, on grounds of religion, an act is *de facto* a crime or offense against public order. But this happens only when the act either injures the rights of others, or violates common public morality, or gravely disturbs the public peace. In these cases the right of public authority to restrain the use of freedom for the preservation of public order is verified, and a person's immunity ceases, inasmuch as he is no longer acting in a manner that is consonant with personal dignity.

8. *Conclusion.* Man's right to freedom in matters of religion is based on the objective truth of the dignity of the human person, and on the objectively true principles derived therefrom, which have to do with the right ordering of society.

IV. Objections Raised against the Declaration

1. With regard to its *method.* Another method is sometimes proposed: the discussion of religious freedom should begin with the doctrine on conscience, showing the distinction between a true and an erroneous conscience.

This suggested method does not seem to fit the state of the question as it is presented today. We are not dealing with the question of whether man has from a true conscience a right to act, a right which he does not have from an erroneous conscience. It is rather a question of a human right, in the sense that a right affirms an immunity from coercion. More precisely, it is a question of whether, and under what conditions, there is a right on the part of others, and particularly on the part of public authority, to prevent a man from acting in public according to his own conscience. From the fact that one is acting with an erroneous conscience it does not follow that others have the right to prevent his action. No human authority has any competence to pass judgment on whether a man's conscience is true or erroneous, whether it was rightly formed or wrongly, "for that is in the power of God alone, who alone searches and judges the secret designs of the heart" *(Pacem in terris, op. cit.,* p. 270).

2. With regard to the *arguments.* In the present state of the question it is futile to cite the principle that rights are not equally based on truth and on error. This is indeed true if it means that a right is not founded on error, but only on truth. But again, one must take into consideration that today it is a question about a right as an immunity from coercion. Of course, a man with a true conscience enjoys that immunity, but so also does a man with an erroneous conscience until it is proved that someone else, and particularly civil authority, has in the particular case the right to impede this or that external act of religion.

It is also futile in the present state of the question to adduce the other principle that it is wrong for civil authority to hold truth and error as of equal right. This indeed is valid principle, but it does not apply in the matter under discussion, for it is not at all a matter of the State's passing judgment on truth and error in matters of religion. It is simply a matter of preserving a person's immunity when acting in public in accordance with his own conscience, unless his action happens to be an offense against public order.

Furthermore, in no sense whatever is it stated in the Declaration that the man with a true conscience and the man with an erroneous conscience are in equal or like condition either morally or spiritually. That would be absurd. Again, it is a matter only of their juridical status in human society, in which they ought to enjoy the same equal civil rights, in view of the fact that "all men are equal by reason of their natural dignity" (*Pacem in terris, op. cit.,* p. 268).

It is also worth mentioning that the Declaration does not assert there is any right to spread religious errors in society. Such a claim, both in itself and especially in the present state of the question, has no meaning. More precisely, the question under discussion is whether and by what right civil authority can restrain, by the use of force, a man who is giving public witness to his religious beliefs. When the question is put in this way, the old principle again asserts itself that it is not the business of civil authority to pass judgment on religious truth or error, although that authority does have the duty to refrain from coercive action, unless it can be proved that a public offense is involved in the circumstances.

3. With regard to the *norm of law*. The opinion is advanced that civil intolerance (or the use of force to prevent men from acting publicly in accordance with their conscience) must be exercised whenever it is necessary to allow it. But this opinion seems to be based on premises that cannot be proved. It supposes an absolute moral principle: error in matters of faith and morals must always be repressed when such repression is possible, and such error must not to be tolerated except when tolerance is necessary. But this, it would seem, can hardly be reconciled with the teaching of Pope

Pius XII in *Ci riesce* (cf. above, p. 118). Likewise, one can hardly reconcile with the norm of law the opinion that in matters of religion as much force must be used as is possible, and only as much freedom allowed as is necessary.

4. With regard to *tolerance on the part of the State*. Only those evils are said to be tolerated which are adjudged by competent authority to be evils. But a policy of religious freedom in society can in no way be regarded as an evil, since it has its foundation in the very dignity of the human person and constitutes an essential element of the common good of society. Therefore, one cannot speak of such a policy as being "tolerated", whether by society in general, or by the State, or by individual citizens.

Error in religious matters is indeed in itself something evil, which God himself only tolerates, and therefore men too ought merely to tolerate it. But tolerance in this sense is a moral concept. It denotes an attitude of mind, informed with both truth and prudence, toward what is known to be something evil, but which must, for valid reasons, be permitted. But one may not, on that account, translate tolerance of religious error into a juridical concept, by which the State itself would have to be guided in its activity. For the State is not an authority competent to pass judgment on truth or error in matters of religion. Therefore, one cannot speak of error in religion being "tolerated" by the State.

It is sometimes alleged that religious errors, especially when publicly proclaimed in a uniformly Catholic country, are harmful to the common good. Even granting that charge, it does not follow that civil authority must forcibly restrain those errors or cults in some way founded upon error. For, on the one hand, it is not the duty of the State to eliminate, either by law or by any other coercive measure, everything that is in any way opposed to the common good. On the other hand, it is assuredly the duty of the State to protect the rights or immunities of the human person in matters of religion, except, of course, when these cease to hold, on account of a violation of public order.

Furthermore, it is for the Church alone to be able to exhort in sound doctrine and to confute opponents (cf. Tit. 1, 9) so that men will not be deceived by philosophy and vain deceit, according to human traditions and according to the elements of the world (cf. Col. 2, 8).

5. With regard to *diversity of circumstances*. The relation between the Church and all other societies with their duly constituted civil authorities is not, and even need not be, unique or univocal. For that relationship must be determined on the basis of historical and sociological circumstances, as the Declaration implies. But it is entirely wrong to assert that the demands of the dignity of the human person, as well as the rights of man, are not identical in a "confessional State" and in a "pluralistic society".

6. With regard to *the basis of the right*. True, a right cannot be founded on error, but only on truth. But the rights of a person are based upon that objective truth—the dignity of the person—and upon the objective truths that are the principles flowing from that dignity according to which society must be ordered. But ultimately those rights are founded upon the whole objective moral order (cf. St. Thomas, *Contra Gentes,* III, 129), and the dignity of the human person is one of its essential elements.

V. The Subject and Nature of Rights

Frequently reference is made to "the rights of truth", or to the "right to truth", and the "right to be wrong". In the interests of clarity, therefore, it will be of benefit to explain briefly the common teaching on the subject of rights and the nature of that subject.

Only physical or moral persons are the subject of rights. A right, therefore, immediately and formally connotes an intersubjective relation, a relation, that is, between a person and a person. For in every juridical relationship there are involved two persons or two subjects; there is the active subject in whom the right exists, and the passive subject who is obliged to render the object of that right, either by an action or by the omission of an action. In the strict sense, therefore, there is no right to truth, for the relation between a person and the truth is either a logical or a moral relation, but not a juridical relation. There can be, and is, a right that one not be prevented by another from speaking the truth. But in this case the object of the right is not the manifestation of the truth; it is rather what the passive subject of the right is obliged to render, and that is immunity from coercion or the omission of an action which would impede the truth from being spoken by the active subject of the right.

Certainly there can at times be a right that someone speak or teach the truth: for example, when it is a matter of witnesses testifying in trials, or of teachers in schools. But even in these cases there is no juridical relation between the person and the truth; however, there is a relation between the person (the active subject of the right) in whom inheres the right that the truth be told or taught, and the person (passive subject of the right) who has the correlative duty to speak or to teach the truth. And if the truth is not spoken or is not taught, there is no harm done to the rights of the undeclared truth, but there is an injury to the right of the person to whom the truth should have been manifested. In these circumstances there has indeed been an offense against truth, but this is a moral irregularity, and not an injury to a right.

It is quite evident, however, that there is not and cannot be a right to error; this would be senseless. But there can be, and is, a right not to be impeded by others, by use of coercive means, from putting into effect what is erroneous or from communicating it to others. This is the sense in which the word "right" is taken in the Declaration.

VI. The Nature of the State

There is no reason to fear that the Declaration will appear to favor an "a-religious" or "indifferent" State.

The Declaration is based on traditional teaching regarding the distinction between the two spheres of human life and activity, namely, the sacred and the profane, the civil and the religious. In modern times, this doctrine has been magnificently developed and enlarged by Pope Leo XIII. He taught more clearly than ever was done before that there are two societies, two systems of law, and two authorities, both divinely established but in different ways, that is, by the natural law and the positive law of Christ. As the policy of religious freedom is based on this distinction of orders, so also is it a certain means of religiously maintaining that distinction against the confusions which history has often engendered.

The Declaration is also based on another distinction which especially Pope Pius XII and Pope John XXIII have highly praised. This is the distinction between society and the State.

First of all, a policy of religious freedom, so far from being harmful to religion in society, is rather highly advantageous to it. This is evident to anyone who carefully reads the Declaration, nn. 6-7 (the protection and promotion of religion in society) and also nn. 12-13 (how the Church is able to carry out its mission effectively, and its faithful is able to live a Christian life). Furthermore, society itself is free, so that it can have acts of public worship by which society, as such, can acknowledge its dependence on God and pay him the honor that is due to him, in fulfillment of a duty that is incumbent upon society as such.

Secondly, the notion of religious freedom in no way implies that the State is or ought to be a-religious or indifferent to religion. The principle itself is evident: it is the duty of the State *ex officio* to have some concern for religion. That is to say, the State is bound to be favorably inclined toward religion in the manner that is proper for it, and to the greatest extent possible, in keeping with its earthly and temporal character. For where the State with its authority recognizes and protects a policy of religious freedom, all its citizens are free in seeking, embracing, giving witness to and living religious truth. This too is a function, by no means to be despised, which the State performs for human persons in society. Furthermore, in its protection of religious freedom the State also acknowledges the high social value of religion itself; the cultivation of such a value by the citizens brings about many advantages both for society and the State, as is explicitly stated (n. 6). One can hardly object, then, that by protecting religious freedom the State is showing itself to be indifferent toward the various religions, whether these are true or false. For, in so doing, the State is protecting not religious indifferentism, but rather the dignity of the human person and his rights.

VII. THE CONCEPT OF PUBLIC ORDER

This is a concept recognized in canon law: "Travelers are not bound by the laws of the place in which they happen to be, excepting such laws as are concerned with public order. . . ." (can. 14, §1, n. 2). This concept is thus explained by Vermeersch: "The words 'public order' are not sufficiently defined from the mind of the legislator, and are interpreted according to accepted usages. Authors are sufficiently agreed that laws concerned with public order are those which have the public or common good not only for their end (as does every law), but for their immediate object. If such laws are not observed by everyone in a given territory, the community itself will suffer harm. Such laws are not those that aim at promoting the sanctification of the faithful. It might perhaps be said that public order is protected by laws made for the purpose of avoiding harm, rather than for the advancement of the common good. Travelers, *per se*, do not have to cooperate for the common good of an alien territory, since they do not belong to that particular community; yet they may be prevented from being harmful to it."

Therefore, the distinction between the common good and public order is consistent with the now well-known distinction between society and the State. The *bene esse* of society is one thing, and something that every society is bound to preserve; but the *esse* itself of society is another thing, and this the State is bound to ensure. Now, to the *bene esse* of society pertain all those goods of any kind that have to do with the perfection of the human person here on earth. But to the *esse* itself of society pertain the political good, which is public peace, the moral good, which is public morality, and the good of justice, which is the secure possession and exercise of human and civil rights.

Therefore, what is useful for society is one thing, but what is necessary for it is something else. Likewise, what is opposed to public order is one thing, and something to be repressed, but what is opposed to the common good is something else, and something not necessarily to be repressed, since *per se* the principle of freedom is valid and established by the norm of law. Granting all this, one can see why the demands of public order justify a restriction of freedom in a particular case, and, at the same time, why the advantages to the common good would not justify such a restriction. It is because the former have a special urgency, whereas the latter do not. As Vermerrsch says, a restriction of liberty may be legitimate for the sake of avoiding harm, but never for the sake of promoting the common good. The widest civil liberty is of importance to the common good itself, because that liberty is by nature suited to bring about progress in life and the perfecting of the human person.

Lastly, it is not true that the Declaration defends an obsolete concept of the so-called liberalist State (police State), for, according to the old axiom, abstracting is not lying. But the Declaration had to abstract or prescind from a great many more general questions concerning the State's intervention in social life, as, for example, of what kind and how extensive such intervention can and ought to be. The document does touch briefly on the principle of positive subsidies which the State can offer toward the more ready exercise of religion in society. But this is a complicated question, and judgment should be made according to different political traditions and varying sociological circumstances, and not by an *a priori* method.

APPENDIX III

The Declaration on Religious Freedom *

by

John Courtney Murray, S.J.

The *Declaration on Religious Freedom* is a
document of very modest scope. It is concerned only
with the juridico-social order and with the validity,
in that order, of a human and civil right to the
free exercise of religion. The right is founded on
the dignity of the human person; its essential requirement is that man in society should be free
from all constraint or hindrance, whether legal or
extra-legal, in what concerns religious belief, worship, witness and practice, both private and public. The structure of a rational argument for this
right is briefly sketched; norms for legitimate limitation of the exercise of the right are laid down; the
duty of government to protect and foster the free
exercise of religion in society is affirmed. Then the
implications of religious freedom for all Churches
and religious communities are set forth in some
detail. Thereafter the human right to religious
freedom is considered under the light of revelation.

---

* This article, printed here in its entirety, appeared in
Concilium 15: *War, Poverty, Freedom* (Glen Rock, New Jersey: Paulist Press [1966], pp. 3-16).

The intention of this section is simply to show that a harmony exists between religious freedom in the juridico-social sense, and Christian freedom in the various senses of this latter concept as they emerge from scripture and from the doctrine of the Church. The Declaration merely suggests that the two kinds of freedom are related; it does not undertake to specify more closely what their precise relationship is. The conclusion of the Declaration is a pastoral exhortation to the faithful and a respectful appeal to the conscience of mankind, urging the value of religious freedom, and of religion itself, in the world today.

The Declaration therefore does not undertake to present a full and complete theology of freedom. This would have been a far more ambitious task. It would have been necessary, I think, to develop four major themes: (1) the concept of Christian freedom—the freedom of the People of God—as a participation in the freedom of the Holy Spirit, the principal agent in the history of salvation, by whom the children of God are "led" (Rom. 8, 14) to the Father through the incarnate Son; (2) the concept of the freedom of the Church in her ministry, as a participation in the freedom of Christ himself, to whom all authority in heaven and on earth was given and who is present in his Church to the end of time (cf. Matt. 28, 18. 20); (3) the concept of Christian faith as man's free response to the divine call issued, on the Father's eternal and gracious initiative, through Christ, and heard by man in his heart where the Spirit speaks what he has himself heard (cf. John 16, 13-15); (4) the juridical concept of religious freedom as a human and civil right, founded on the native dignity of the human person who is made in the image of God and therefore enjoys, as his birthright, a participation in the freedom of God himself.

This would have been, I think, a far more satisfactory method of procedure, from the theological point of view. In particular, it would have been in conformity with the disposition of theologians today to view issues of natural law within the concrete context of the present historico-existential order of grace. Moreover, the doctrine presented would have been much richer in content. There were, however, decisive reasons why the Council could not undertake to present this full theology of freedom.

1. The Declaration is the only conciliar document that is formally addressed to the world at large on a topic of intense secular as well as religious interest. Therefore, it would have been inept for the Declaration to begin with doctrines that can be known only by revelation and accepted only by faith.

2. What the world at large, as well as the faithful within the Church, wants to know today is the stand of the Church on religious freedom as a human and civil right. It would be idle to deny that the doctrine of the Church, as formulated in the 19th century, is somewhat ambiguous in itself, out of touch with contemporary reality and a cause of confusion among the faithful and of suspicion throughout large sectors of public opinion.

3. The theological structure of the argument, as proposed above, would give rise to historical and theological problems which are still matters of dispute among theologians. There is, for instance, the problem of the exact relationship between Christian freedom and religious freedom. There is, furthermore, the whole problem of the develop-

ment of doctrine, from *Mirari vos* to *Dignitatis humanae personae.*

4. Christian freedom, as the gift of the Holy Spirit, is not exclusively the property of the members of the visible Church, any more than the action of the Spirit is confined within the boundaries of the visible Church. This topic is of great ecumenical importance, but the discussion of it would have to be nice in every respect, and therefore impossible in a brief document.

5. Finally, there was a serious consideration of pastoral prudence. Christian freedom is indeed asserted over against all earthly powers (cf. Acts 4, 19-20; 5, 29); in this sense it prompted the witness of the martyrs. It is, however, also asserted within the Church; in this sense it is the warrant for charismatic ministries, and it is also the basis of prudent protest when the exercise of authority goes beyond legitimate bounds. As everyone knows, however, the issue of freedom within the Church is neuralgic today, as indeed it was when Paul wrote to the Galatians (cf. Gal. 5, 13). The issue is also highly complicated. It would have been imprudent, therefore, to raise this issue directly in a brief conciliar document. Hence the Declaration is at pains to distinguish sharply the issue of religious freedom in the juridico-social order from the larger issue of Christian freedom. The disastrous thing would be to confuse the two distinct issues. Obviously, the issue of Christian freedom—its basis, its meaning, its exercise and its limits—will have to be clarified by free discussion, conducted carefully and patiently in a sustained dialogue between pastors and people over many years. However, this dialogue will be the more successful now that the Declaration has settled the lesser issue of the free exercise of religion in civil society.

Narrow though its scope may be, the Declaration is nonetheless a document of considerable theological significance. This will become apparent if the document is considered in the light of the two great historical movements of the 19th century, both of which were bitterly opposed by the Church.

I
THE SECULARITY OF SOCIETY AND STATE

The first movement was from the sacral conception of society and State to the secular conception. The sacral conception had been the heritage of medieval Christendom and, in a far more ambiguous form, of the ancien régime. For our purposes here, two of its characteristics should be briefly noted. First, the Christian world—or at least the Catholic nation—was considered to be somehow enclosed within the Church, which was herself the one Great Society. Second, the religious prerogative of the prince extended to a care of the religion of his subjects and a care of their religious unity as essential to their political unity. (This religious prerogative of political rule was interpreted in a variety of more or less arbitrary ways, but these details need not detain us here.)

The 19th century saw the break with this conception of the sacrality of society and State, and a movement toward their secularity. As everybody knows, the Church—both in Rome and in the so-called Catholic nations—opposed this movement with all the forces at her command. The reason was obvious. After the revolution in continental Europe (the new Federal Republic of the United States presents an altogether different case), the term of the historical movement was not a proper secularity of society and State. What emerged was the laicized State of rationalist or atheist inspiration, whose function was the laicization of society. In effect, what emerged was the ancien régime turned upside down, as Alexis de Tocqueville noted at the time. One might properly regard the Law of Separation (December 9, 1905) of the Third French Republic as the legislative symbol of the new order.

The Church could not in principle accept this new order in its premises, in its ethos, or even in its institutions, primary among which was the institution of the so-called "liberty of cult". Furthermore, the Church did not in fact do a work of discernment of the signs of the times in order to discover, beneath the transitory historical forms assumed by the new movement, the true and valid dynamisms that were at work.

The overt revolt was against the sacrality of society and State as symbolized by the union of throne and altar. Few historians today would deny that this conception and its institutional symbol, for all their venerable antiquity, had become archaistic in the world of modernity. However, the true underlying direction of the new movement was toward a proper and legitimate secularity of society and State. In the depths, where the hidden factors of historical change were operative, what what was really going on was a work of differentiation, which is always a work of growth and progress. Civil society was seeking differentation from the religious community, the Church. The political functions of secular rule were being differentiated from the religious functions of ecclesiastical authority. The trouble was that this work of orderly progress was disrupted and deflected, as so often happens in history.

Chiefly to blame was the disastrous law of contradiction—that desire to deny and destroy the past which was the very essence of Enlightenment rationalism (whereby it aroused the bitter antipathy, for instance, of Edmund Burke). What appeared on the surface, therefore, was not progress but simply revolution. Society as civil was not simply being differentiated from society as religious; the two societies were being violently separated, and civil society was being stripped of all religious substance. The order of civil law and political jurisdiction was not simply being differentiated from the order of moral law and ecclesiastical jurisdiction; a complete rupture was made between the two orders of law and the two authorities, and they were set at hostile variance, each with the other. Society and State were not invested with their due secularity; they were roughly clothed in the alien garments of continental laicism. At this horrid specter, stalking across the Europe of the Middle Ages, the Church in the person of Pius IX hurled her unmitigated anathema.

Leo XIII first began to discern whither the deep currents of history were setting. In response, he restored to its proper centrality, and also developed, the traditional truth that Gelasius I had sought to enforce upon the Emperor Anastasius in 494 A.D.: "Two there are, august Emperor, whereby this world is ruled by sovereign right (*principaliter*), the sacred authority of the priesthood and the royal power." However, Leo XIII transcended the historically conditioned medieval conception of the two powers in the one society called Christendom—a conception that, in debased form, had persisted under the ancien régime, with its Gallicanism and its famous device: "One faith, one law, one king." In a series of eight splendid texts, stretching from *Arcanum* (1880) to *Pervenuti* (1902), Leo XIII finally made it clear that there are two distinct societies, two distinct orders of law, as well as two distinct powers. This was the ancient affirmation in a new mode of understanding—an authentic development of doctrine. On this basis, Leo XIII was able to accomplish a second development. In scores of texts—more than a hundred in all, of which about one-fourth had to do with the Roman Question—he reiterated that the essential claim which the Church makes on civil societies and their governments is stated in the ancient formula, "the freedom of the Church". It was not possible for him to complete these two developments with a third—the affirmation of the freedom of society and of the duty of governments toward the freedom of the people. In any event, his doctrinal work cleared the way for further progress in understanding the rightful secularity of society and State, as against the ancient sacral conceptions.

This progress reaches its inevitable term in the *Declaration on Religious Freedom.* The sacrality of society and State is now transcended as archaistic. Government is not *defensor fidei.* Its duty and rights do not extend to what had long been called *cura religionis,* a direct care of religion itself and of the unity of the Church within Christendom or the nation-state. The function of government is secular: that is, it is confined to a care of the free exercise of religion within society —a care therefore of the freedom of the Church and of the freedom of the human person in religious affairs. The function is secular because freedom in society, for all that it is most precious to religion and the Church, remains a secular value

—the sort of value that government can protect and foster by the instrument of law. Moreover, to this conception of the State as secular, there corresponds a conception of society itself as secular. It is not only distinct from the Church in its origin and finality; it is also autonomous in its structures and processes. Its structural and dynamic principles are proper to itself and proper to the secular order—the truth about the human person, the justice due to the human person, the love that is the properly human bond among persons and, not least, the freedom that is the basic constituent and requirement of the dignity of the person.

This is the true Christian understanding of society and State in their genuine secularity which appears in *Pacem in terris*. The *Declaration on Religious Freedom* adds to it the final clarity in the essential detail, namely, that in the secular society, under the secular State, the highest value that both State and society are called upon to protect and foster is the personal and social value of the free exercise of religion. The values of religion itself for men and society are to be protected and fostered by the Church and by other religious communities availing themselves of their freedom. Thus the Declaration assumes its primary theological significance. Formally, it settles only the minor issue of religious freedom. In effect, it defines the Church's basic contemporary view of the world—of human society, of its order of human law and of the functions of the all too human powers that govern it. Therefore, the Declaration not only completes the *Decree on Ecumenism*, it also lays down the premise, and sets the focus, of the Church's concern with the secular world, which is the subject of Chapter XIII. Not nostalgic yearnings to restore ancient sacralizations, not futile efforts to find new forms of sacralizing the terrestrial and temporal order in its structures and processes, but the purification of these processes and structures and the sure direction of them to their inherently secular ends—this is the aim and object of the action of the Church in the world today.

In its own way, the Declaration is an act in that lengthy process known today as *consecratio mundi*. The document makes clear that the statute of religious freedom as a civil right is, in reality, a self-denying ordinance on the part of government. Secular government denies to itself the right to interfere with the free exercise of religion, unless an issue of civil offense against public order arises (in which case the State is acting only in the secular order, not in the order of religion). On the other hand, the ratification of the Declaration by Vatican Council II is, with equal clarity, a self-denying ordinance on the part of the Church. To put the matter simply and in historical perspective, the Church finally renounces, in principle, its long-cherished historical right to *auxilium brachii saecularis* (the phrase in Canon 2198 remains for the moment an odd bit of archaism). The secular arm is simply secular, inept for the furtherance of the proper purposes of the People of God. More exactly, the Church has no secular arm. In ratifying the principle of religious freedom, the Church accepts the full burden of the freedom which is the single claim she is entitled to make on the secular world. Thus a lengthy, twisting, often tortuous development of doctrine comes to a term.

Like all developments, this one will initiate a further progress in doctrine, that is, a new *impostazione* of the doctrine of the Church on the problem of Church and State, as it is called, in order to restore, and to perfect in its own sense, the authentic tradition. This, however, is a subject in itself, not to be dealt with here.

II
HISTORICAL CONSCIOUSNESS

The second great trend of the 19th century was the movement from classicism to historical consciousness. The meaning of these two terms would require lengthy explanation, both historical and philosophical. Suffice it to say here that classicism designates a view of truth which holds objective truth, precisely because it is objective, to exist "already out there now" (to use Bernard Lonergan's descriptive phrase). Therefore, it also exists apart from its possession by anyone. In addition, it exists apart from history, formulated in propositions that are verbally immutable. If there is to be talk of development of doctrine, it can only mean that the truth, remaining itself unchanged in its formulation, may find different applications in the contingent world of historical change. In contrast, historical consciousness, while holding fast to the nature of truth as objective, is concerned with the possession of truth, with man's affirmations of truth, with the understanding contained in these affirmations, with the conditions—both circumstantial and subjective—of understanding and affirmation, and therefore with the historicity of truth and with progress in the grasp and penetration of what is true.

The Church in the 19th century, and even in the 20th, opposed this movement toward historical consciousness. Here, too, the reason was obvious. The term of the historical movement was modernism, that "conglomeration of all heresies", as *Pascendi dominici gregis* called it. The insight into the historicity of truth and the insight into the role of the subject in the possession of truth were systematically exploited to produce almost every kind of pernicious "ism", unto the destruction of the notion of truth itself—its objective character, its universality, its absoluteness. These systematizations were false, but the insights from which they issued were valid. Here again a work of discernment needed to be done, and was not done. To be quite summary about it, this work had to wait until Vatican Council II. (I am not here speaking of the work of scholars.)

The sessions of the Council have made it clear that, despite resistance in certain quarters, classicism is giving way to historical consciousness. Obviously, neither of these theories has been debated, and perhaps they are not even understood as theories. The significant thing is that the Council has chosen to call itself "pastoral". The term has been misunderstood, as if the Council were somehow not concerned with truth and doctrine but only with life and practical directives for living. To so contrast the pastoral and doctrinal would be disastrous. The pastoral concern of the Council is a doctrinal concern. However, it is illuminated by historical consciousness: that is, by concern for the truth not simply as a proposition to be repeated but more importantly as a possession to be lived; by concern, therefore, for the subject to whom the truth is addressed; hence, also, by concern for the historical moment in which the truth is proclaimed to the living subject; and, consequently, by concern to seek that progress in the understanding of the truth demanded both by the historical moment and by the subject who must live in it. In a word, the fundamental concern of the Council is with the development of doctrine. The scholarly concern of the 20th century has become also the pastoral concern of the Church in 20th century.

Viewed in this light, the second theological significance of the *Declaration on Religious Freedom* appears. The Declaration is a pastoral exercise in the development of doctrine. (This, it may be said in passing, is why it met some opposition; classicism—if not as a theory, at least as an operative mentality—is still with us, here and there.) Briefly, the Declaration bases itself on a progress in doctrine that has, in fact, occurred since Leo XIII. It also carries this progress one inevitable step further by discarding an older theory of civil tolerance in favor of a new doctrine of religious freedom more in harmony with the authentic and more fully understood tradition of the Church. Only a bare outline of this progress can be suggested here.

The remote theological premise of the Declaration is the traditional teaching of the Church, clarified by Leo XIII, with regard to the two orders of human life, the sacred and the secular, the civil and the religious. The immediate premise is the philosophy of society and its juridical organization —in this sense, a philosophy of the State—developed by Pius XII and given a more systematic statement by John XXIII in *Pacem in terris*. This philosophy is deeply rooted in tradition; it is also, by comparison with Leo XIII, new.

The Leonine doctrine, more Aristotelian and medieval in inspiration, rested on the conception of the common good as an ensemble of social virtues and values, chiefly the value of obedience to the laws. The Pian and Joannine doctrine, more profoundly Christian in inspiration, rests on the conception of the common good as consisting chiefly in the effective exercise of the rights, and the faithful discharge of the duties, of the human person. Correlatively, in the Leonine conception the function of government was primarily ethical, namely, the direction of the citizen-subject—who was considered more subject than citizen—toward the life of virtue by the force of good laws reflecting the demands of the moral order. In the Pian and Joannine doctrine, on the other hand, the primary function of government is juridical, namely, the protection and promotion of the exercise of human and civil rights, and the facilitation of the discharge of human and civil duties by the citizen who is fully citizen, that is, not merely subject to, but also participant in, the processes of government.

The insight of Pius XII, which lay at the root of the new development, was stated thus: "Man as such, so far from being regarded as the object of social life or a passive element thereof, is rather to be considered its subject, foundation and end." In contrast, the customary focus of Leo XIII's doctrine was on the *principes* (his favorite word), the rulers who wielded in society the power they had received from God. In this latter conception, society is to be built and rendered virtuous from the top down, as it were; the role of government is dominant. In the former conception, however, society is to be built and rendered virtuous from the bottom up, as it were; the role of government is subordinate, a role of service to the human person. Moreover, in Leo XIII's conception (except in *Rerum novarum*), government was not only personal but paternal; the "prince" was *pater patriae*, as society was the family writ large. In Pius XII's conception, on the other hand, government is simply political; the relation between ruler and ruled is a civil relation, not familial. This was a return to tradition (notably to Aquinas), after the aberrations of continental absolutism and the exaggerations of the Roman-law jurists.

Leo XIII's paternal conception owed much to historical fact and to the political culture of his day. The pivotal fact was the *imperita multitudo,* the illiterate formless masses which reappear time and again in his text. In contrast, Pius XII's political conception was a return to tradition, to the noble idea of "the people", a structured concept at whose root stands, as he said, "the citizen [who] feels within himself the consciousness of his own personality, of his duties and rights, and of his due freedom as joined with a respect for the freedom and dignity of others". This return to the tradition of "the free man under a limited government" (as someone has summarized the basic political insight of Aquinas) was likewise a progress in the understanding of the tradition.

Finally, in Leo XIII the traditional distinction between society and State was largely lost from view; its disappearance from history had been, in fact, part of the *damnosa haereditas*—the fateful heritage—of the ancien régime. It is a noteworthy fact that nowhere in the immense body of Leo XIII's writings is there to be found a satisfactory philosophy of human law and jurisprudence. He was always the moralist, not the jurist. His concern was to insist that the juridical order of society must recognize the imperatives of the objective moral order. This emphasis was indeed necessary against the moral antinomianism and juridical positivism of continental laicism. However, in consequence of this polemic necessity, Leo XIII gave little if any attention to the internal structure of the juridical order itself—the structure, that is, of the State.

This became the preoccupation of Pius XII, as the menace of totalitarianism loomed large, threatening the basic dignity of the human person, which is his freedom. Pius XII revived the distinction between society and State, the essential barrier against totalitarianism. He also made it a pillar of his concept of the juridical State (the phrase is alien in English; we speak of "constitutional government"). The powers of government are not only limited to the terrestrial and temporal order. Since Leo XIII this had been clear doctrine, however much it may have been disregarded in practice. But even within this limited order, the powers of government are limited by the higher order of human rights, defined in detail in *Pacem in terris,* whose doctrine is completed by the *Declaration on Religious Freedom.* The safekeeping and promotion of these rights is government's first duty to the common good.

Even this rapid comparison may help to make clear that, although Leo XIII's theory of civil tolerance was coherent with his conception of society and State, it is not coherent with the more fully developed philosophy of Pius XII and John XXIII. For Leo XIII the power of the ruler was *patria potestas,* a paternal power. The ruler-father can, and is obliged to, know what is true and good —the true religion and the moral law. His primary duty, as father-ruler, is to guide his children-subjects—the illiterate masses—to what is true and good. His consequent function is to protect them against religious error and moral aberration —against the preachments of the "sects" (that favorite Leonine word). The masses are to be regarded as children, *ad instar puerorum,* who are helpless to protect themselves. They must look to the ruler-father, who knows what is true and good and also knows what is good for them. In these circumstances, and given this personal conception of rule, the attitude of government toward what is error and evil could only be one of tolerance. Government permits by law what it cannot prevent by law. Moreover, this civil tolerance is no more than a dictate of necessity; it is practiced for the sake of a greater good—the peace of the community. This theory of civil tolerance may indeed be regarded as a counsel of practical wisdom. It can hardly be regarded as permanent Catholic doctrine, any more than the theory of government, with which it is correlative, may be so regarded. The roots of both theories are in the contingencies of history, not in the exigencies of abiding truth.

Therefore, the *Declaration on Religious Freedom* puts aside the post-Reformation and 19th-century theory of civil tolerance. The fault is not error but archaism. A new philosophy of society and State has been elaborated, more transtemporal in its manner of conception and statement, less time-conditioned, more differentiated, a progress in the understanding of the tradition. Briefly, the structural elements of this philosophy are the four principles of social order stated, and developed in their exigencies, in *Pacem in terris*—the principles of truth, justice, love and freedom. The declaration of the human and civil right to the free exercise of religion is not only in harmony with, but also required by, these four principles. The foundation of the right is the truth of human dignity. The object of the right—freedom from coercion in religious matters—is the first debt due in justice to the human person. The final motive for respect of the right is a love and appreciation of the personal dignity of man. Religious freedom itself is the first of all freedoms in a well-organized society, without which no other human and civil freedoms can be safe.

APPENDIX IV

The Declaration on Religious Freedom of Vatican Council II and statements of the World Council of Churches show a convergence of articulate agreement and reveal the problems of religious freedom still existing for all Christian Churches.

In Part One of this Appendix, Fr. Stransky gives a short background to the WCC statements, which are cited in full. In Part II, Dr. Lukas Vischer, Secretary of the WCC Commission on Faith and Order, compares the Declaration on Religious Freedom with WCC thinking.

Part One

The Declaration and the World Council of Churches

The World Council of Churches (WCC) was organized in 1948, at a time of critical international strain and of totalitarian hostility to the Christian faith, which in a number of countries had led to persecution of the Churches and, in some instances, to the proscription of public worship and other normal religious activities.

The Assembly called to organize the WCC convened at Amsterdam in August, 1948. A section on "The Church and the International Disorder" submitted for the approval of the Assembly *A Declaration on Religious Liberty,* in which is described freedom of religion—"an essential element in a good international order". In brief, this Declaration stated:

1. "Every person has the right to determine his own faith and creed."

2. "Every person has the right to express his religious beliefs in worship, teaching and practice, and to proclaim the implications of his beliefs for relationships in a social or political community."

3. "Every person has the right to associate with others and to organize with them for religious purposes."

4. "Every religious organization, formed or maintained by action in accordance with the rights of individual persons, has the right to determine its policies and practices for the accomplishment of its chosen purposes."

A few months after the Amsterdam statement the General Assembly of the United Nations, meeting in Paris, adopted the *Universal Declaration of Human Rights* (Dec. 10, 1948).

After declaring that "everyone is entitled to all the rights and freedoms set forth in this Declaration without distinction of any kind, such as race, color, sex, language, political or other opinion, national or social origin, property, birth or other status" (Article 2), the U.N. document states (Article 18):

"Everyone has the right to freedom of thought, conscience and religion; this right includes freedom to change his religion or belief, and freedom, either alone or in community with others and in private or public, to manifest his religion or belief in teaching, practice, worship and observance."

After Amsterdam, the WCC Commission of the Churches on International Affairs (CCIA) continued to study the religious liberty question and offer practical suggestions to the member Churches. The Second Assembly (Evanston, Ill., August, 1954) noted "a number of specific and serious cases of religious persecution and repression", reaffirmed the Amsterdam Declaration, called attention to the U.N. statement and instructed the CCIA "to continue to use every effort in representations to the governments concerned and, where they are involved, the religious authorities".

In 1957, the WCC Central Committee instructed the Executive Committee "to arrange for studies to be made of the problem of religious liberty in the Roman Catholic and other countries"—a resolution that did not set well with some Roman Catholic commentators.

Then in January, 1959, Pope John XXIII announced Vatican Council II. The WCC Executive Committee that summer emphasized that relations between the Roman Catholic Church and other Churches "could be greatly improved if opportunity were given for greater cooperation in social service and in working for just and durable peace, if there could be more discussion among theologians, and *if the Churches would join in securing full religious liberty for all peoples in all lands.*"

A year later Pope John set up the Secretariat for Promoting Christian Unity, and the Executive Committee welcomed the fact "that a dialogue with the Roman Catholic Church becomes possible"; the WCC would make known to the Secretariat "certain basic convictions which have been expressed by the Assembly or the Central Committee (e.g., *issues of religious liberty,* Christian social action, etc.)". In May, 1961, an informal and unpublicized consultation on religious freedom was held between Roman Catholic and WCC experts. Msgr. Jan Willebrands, Secretary of the Unity Secretariat and Fr. Jerome Hamer, O.P., one of its consultors, participated.

Following the Second Assembly at Evanston, the Central Committee appointed a commission "to study further proselytism and religious liberty"; certain churches in the WCC, the Orthodox in particular, had from the beginning of the WCC been asking for an end to proselytizing activities. This study was submitted to the Third Assembly which met in New Delhi in December, 1961.

Report on Christian Witness, Proselytism and Religious Liberty in the Setting of the World Council of Churches

As our study has proceeded, it has become increasingly clear that the poles of our problem are to be found in the right and duty of free Christian witness on the one hand, and in the obligation of an ecumenical fellowship to manifest the visible unity of the Church as the body of Christ on the other hand. The tension is between the two, and our problem is to deal justly with both in truth and love.

Consequently, this is a modest and limited report. It attempts not so much to resolve the basic issues as to clarify the nature of the tension and to suggest some guiding principles with regard to the spirit and nature of the relationships within which the Churches may best deal with the issues. Specific rules cannot be prescribed for all national and local situations. Churches which live together are therefore encouraged to strive to achieve mutual understanding, earnestly taking into consideration the ecumenical perspective of this report.

While this report is primarily concerned with relations between the member Churches of the World Council, we are not unmindful of its implication for our relationships with other Churches and religious groups. Our covenant as "Churches which accept our Lord Jesus Christ as God and savior" to "stay together" in brotherly counsel and mutual aid calls for special self-searching in the way we exercise our freedom of witness. But any light we gain as to our right relations with one another is surely relevant to our relations with other Churches.

I. *The Use of the Terms: Christian Witness, Religious Liberty and Proselytism*

Various meanings have been attached to the terms "witness", "religious liberty" and "proselytism". The sense in which we use them in the present discussion needs to be made clear. This is especially true of "proselytism", which today has an almost completely derogatory sense; probably no Church and no missionary society involved in the ecumenical movement would wish to call itself a "proselytizing" body. It does not seem possible, in practice, to restore the good connotation which the word "proselyte" once carried. Thus, "proselytizing" has come to be set over against true obedience to the great commission: "Go therefore and make disciples of all nations, baptizing them in the name of the Father and of the Son and of the Holy Spirit, teaching them to observe all that I have commanded you. . . ." (Mt. 28, 19-20) .

For this true obedience, the words evangelism, apostolate, soul-winning, witness and others are now in common use. In this report the word "witness" will be employed.

(a) *Christian Witness*

Witness in word and deed is the essential mission and responsibility of every Christian and of every Church. All disciples stand under the great commission of the one Lord.

The purpose of witness is to persuade persons to accept the supreme authority of Christ, to commit themselves to him and to render him loving service in the fellowship of his Church. The witness of Christians to Jesus Christ requires both personal and corporate testimony to the truth as it has been revealed to them, but no human testimony to the truth as it is in Jesus Christ can reflect that truth in its fullness. Even when inwardly compelled to testify against that which appears erroneous in some other religious belief or practice, he who would bear a true witness cannot but be humble and honest. He knows but one weight and one measure, the same for himself, as for others.

Such an act of witness seeks a response which contributes to the upbuilding of the fellowship of those who acknowledge the lordship of Christ. A person enters that fellowship by becoming a member of one of the several existing ecclesiastical communities. Both witness and response must therefore, of present necessity, take place within the existing situation of division in the Church.

This situation gives rise to problems in the relationships between the Churches when one Church yields to the temptation to seek its own institutional advantage at the cost of real or seeming disadvantage to another. It is a purpose of the World Council of Churches to help the several Churches so to carry on their witness as to strengthen one another and thus, by their combined effort in mutual cooperation, to spread the Gospel more effectively.

(b) *Religious Liberty*

God's truth and love are given in freedom and call for a free response.

God does not coerce men to respond to his love, and the revelation of God in Christ is a revelation that men are not forced to accept. He calls men to make a willing and obedient response to him in faith, to answer with a free and confident "yes" to the eternal action of his love in which he reveals himself. This utterly free assent is undermined and destroyed when human coercion enters in. Human coercion denies the respect for every individual person which God's loving action in Christ affirms. The non-coercive method and spirit of Christ is in itself the condemnation of all attempts to force men's religious beliefs or to purchase their allegiance, and for the Christian it is the ground of religious liberty.

Every Christian has the liberty, individually or in the corporate body of a Church or other group, to put his whole existence under the authority of God, to believe, pray, worship and proclaim Christ, as well as to live, in accordance with his will, in the Church of his choice according to his own conscience. For such witness and service Churches and individuals should have equality before the law.

It also follows that the conscience of persons whose religious faith and convictions differ from our own must be recognized and respected.

The right of all men to freedom of conscience and freedom of religious belief and practice is recognized by law in most countries. The article on religious liberty in the Universal Declaration of Human Rights is consistent with Christian conviction in this matter: "Everyone has the right to freedom of thought, conscience and religion. This right includes the freedom to change his religion or belief, and freedom, either alone or in community with others, and in public or in private, to manifest his religion or belief in teaching, practice, worship and observance."

(c) "Proselytism"

Proselytism is not something absolutely different from witness: *it is the corruption of witness.* Witness is corrupted when cajolery, bribery, undue pressure or intimidation is used—subtly or openly—to bring about seeming conversion; when we put the success of our Church before the honor of Christ; when we commit the dishonesty of comparing the ideal of our own Church with the actual achievement of another; when we seek to advance our own cause by bearing false witness against another Church; when personal or corporate self-seeking replaces love for every individual soul with whom we are concerned. Such corruption of the Christian witness indicates lack of confidence in the power of the Holy Spirit, lack of respect for the nature of man and lack of recognition of the true character of the Gospel. It is very easy to recognize these faults and sins in others; it is necessary to acknowledge that we are all liable to fall into one or another of them ourselves.

Since the difference between witness and prose-lytism is a matter of purpose, motive and spirit, as well as of means, objective criteria alone cannot adequately distinguish between the two. Neverthe-less, such criteria do exist and *some general objec-tive standards of practice are possible*. The fourth section of this report attempts to describe such standards in the hope that a larger measure of mutual understanding can thereby be attained among the Churches, thus rendering common wit-ness for Christ more faithful and more convinc-ing.

II. *Background*

The issues with which this study is concerned have existed within the ecumenical movement from its very beginning. In 1920 the well-known encyclical of the Ecumenical Patriarchate with its strong plea for cooperation among the Churches asked for a definite cessation of proselytizing activi-ties. When in the same year in Geneva the pre-liminary meetings of "Faith and Order" and of "Life and Work" took place, the issue was again brought up by the Orthodox representatives. In the larger and smaller ecumenical conferences dur-ing the next decades the question was often raised, but no definite action was taken. At the time when the ecclesiological significance of the World Coun-cil of Churches was discussed (Toronto, 1950), this particular aspect of inter-Church relationships was touched upon only very briefly. The Toronto statement says that Churches should "refrain from such actions as are incompatible with brotherly relationships" and develops this point in the following manner: "The positive affirmation of each Church's faith is to be welcomed, but actions incompatible with brotherly relationships toward other member Churches defeat the very purpose for which the Council has been created." * It was, however, not said just what is implied in this constructive relationship.

This extremely brief reference to the history of the discussion shows that these issues call for honest and careful consideration by the member Churches. Failure to deal with them seriously would leave unnecessary misunderstanding in the relationships between member Churches in certain areas.

Behind the issues of "proselytism" and of religious liberty here considered, there lie various historical causes, among which are the following:

1. In the modern age, technological and sociological developments in all parts of our world are radically changing the previously established patterns of human communities. Because means of communication and of mobility have greatly increased, religious and cultural communities no longer find it possible to remain closed to outside influences, but are increasingly being influenced by ideas and movements from outside. It is only necessary to mention the far-reaching influence of newsprint and literature, radio and films, as well as the presence of foreigners and of foreign influences of all types in most countries. National

---

* The complete text of the Toronto statement, "The Ecclesiological Significance of the WCC," is found in Bernard Leeming, S.J., *The Churches and the Church* (Westminster: Newman, 1960), pp. 295–304.

boundary lines cannot any longer isolate a culture. These pervasive and dynamic influences are such that they could only be thwarted by forcible repression—as by cutting off circulation of newsprint and literature, by jamming radio communications and by forbidding free travel and entry into a country.

2. In recent years, religious and cultural communities find themselves extended far beyond their original national and ethnic borders. Refugee resettlement as well as other forms of migration have led to the extension of Orthodox, Protestant and Roman Catholic communities into new territories.

3. In the area of religious and Church relationships the most disturbing situations are found where a particular Church has been historically identified with the total life and culture of a country or territory, whether or not as a legally established or "State Church", and is confronted by religious movements of renewal threatening its unity from within the territory.

The anxiety and resistance manifested by the Church hitherto in sole or dominant occupancy of a territory cannot fairly be ascribed simply to a desire to maintain a privileged monopoly. These may also express a rightful concern for the preservation of the unity and integrity of the Church of the nation and for fidelity to the principle that the Church of the territory has a responsibility for the whole human community in which it is set. Indeed, we are witnessing, especially in Asia and Africa, vigorous efforts to achieve regional or national Church unity. These concerns are often reinforced by nationalist sentiment and the serious desire to preserve the cultural unity of a people.

While it is of the utmost importance that we understand sympathetically these concerns and the real values involved, it is equally important that we recognize the problems they present to religious liberty and the fact that in other parts of the world Churches have found new freedom and vitality in more open and diversified societies.

4. In the 19th century tensions arose out of new contacts between Christians of different Churches in areas taken as fields of foreign missionary activity. In some cases, missions directed toward non-Christians found themselves working among and drawing to themselves members of other Christian Churches already long established in these lands. In other cases, missions were directed toward those who were believed to be lapsed or imperfectly evangelized members of other Churches. At various periods "free Churches" have sprung up or been planted in areas previously the exclusive province of "national Churches" or "State Churches". In recent years there has been a great increase in the number and activity of religious groups appealing for individual conversions, but sometimes with very little Church-consciousness and with little or no interest in cooperation with others.

5. Interacting with these developments and situations is the fact that Churches have become increasingly aware in recent centuries that Christian freedom is at the base of all liberties. Political and social philosophies of the 17th century and after have likewise placed a strong emphasis on liberty in all its forms, including religious liberty.

Churches all over the world find themselves confronted with the necessity of carrying out their mission in a new situation. Many Churches in many areas are troubled by some form of "proselytism".

At the same time the emergence of an organized ecumenical movement has given both a new focal point to the struggle for religious liberty and a new impetus to the claims of unity and fellowship. Our membership together in the World Council of Churches brings us a compelling incentive and an effective instrument for the working out of our new relationship to each other.

III. *Basic Considerations*

1. Every Christian Church is not only permitted but required freely and openly to bear its witness in the world, seeking to bring persons into fellowship with God as revealed in Jesus Christ. Witnessing is a part of the Church's ministry of love, of its service to mankind.

2. The commandment to bear witness to the truth of Christ and to seek to win others to that truth is valid in relation not only to non-Christians but also to others who have no living relationship to any Christian Church. Churches ought to rejoice whenever fresh influences quicken the faith of those committed to their pastoral care, even if those influences come from outside their own structure. Such a quickening witness, brought into the life of a given Church, should be concerned for the unity as well as for the renewal of that Church's life.

3. Should errors or abuses within a Church result in the distorting or obscuring of the central truths of the Gospel and thereby jeopardize men's salvation, other Churches may feel bound to come to the rescue with a faithful witness to the truth thus lost to view. Their liberty to do so must be maintained. But before they undertake

to establish another Church, they must humbly ask themselves whether there are not still to be found in the existing Church such signs of the presence of the Holy Spirit that frank fraternal contact and cooperation with it must be sought.

4. The Toronto Statement of the Central Committee of the World Council of Churches (1950) sets forth some of our present understandings of the ways in which member Churches regard one another:

(a) No Church by virtue of its membership in the World Council (e.g., Toronto Declaration, III, 3, 4 and 5) is under an obligation to suppress, truncate or alter its full confession of truth by which it stands or falls in its being and ministry as a Church, for in so doing it would mutilate itself. It is not in the interest of the World Council to have mutilated Churches as members. On the contrary, it aims to be a Council of whole, real and genuine Churches. This means that every member Church must be able to bring its full untruncated witness of the truth openly and joyfully into the Council and there give it full expression, without holding anything back.

(b) Membership in the World Council does not imply that each Church must regard the other member Churches as Churches in the true and full sense of the word (IV, 4). This means that a Church which in the light of its own confession must regard certain teachings of another member Church as errors and heresies and certain of its practices as abuses cannot be compelled to withdraw or hold back its views because of the Churches' common membership in the World Council, but can and indeed should continue in the future to hold and express its views in their full scope. The more frankly a Church states its views in the Council or within the ecumenical fellowship, the less will be the need to state them in a round-about and undesirable way.

(c) It is precisely within the ecumenical fellowship that this exchange should proceed to the fullest extent and without minimizing the difficulty and seriousness of the issues (cf. IV, 7 and 8). It can be observed that Churches will be most inclined toward proselytism, or, on the other hand, toward making charges of proselytism, when the psychological and spiritual atmosphere is such that Churches either shrink from or are prevented from openly confessing the truth in their relations with each other.

(d) Membership in the World Council places a moral obligation upon the Churches to observe a particular attitude in this discussion. It would be inconsistent with this membership for one member Church altogether to deny another member Church the status of a Church, or to regard it as entirely heretical or hopelessly given over to abuses, so that its members could only be helped by being rescued from it. On the basis of their common confession of Jesus Christ as God and savior and as the one head of the Church, member Churches jointly recognize "hopeful signs" in each other (cf. IV, 1 and 5).

5. Witnessing within the ecumenical fellowship takes place in various ways and the following may be mentioned as examples:

(a) Unofficial discussion and personal encounter between individuals in search of truth.

(b) Official discussion between one Church and another, each giving full weight to its own confession.

(c) An important approach within the framework of the World Council is seen in the work of inter-Church aid, when one Church helps another Church to recover a healthier life of its own; one Church, with the agreement of another, helps it to carry out work of evangelistic, catechetical or educational character or renders some other service on behalf of members of that other Church with the aim not only of leaving them in their own Church, but helping them to be more faithful to it and to become better Christians there. It is clear that this approach demands a great degree of selflessness and humility on the part of both Churches.

IV. *Recommendations for Continuing Consideration by the Member Churches*

During the past several years issues treated in this report have received the consideration of many of the member Churches. The Central Committee of the World Council of Churches has given attention to them at several of its meetings. It is widely recognized that these issues must remain a continuing concern of Churches drawn together, and resolved to stay together, in ecumenical fellowship as member Churches of the World Council. It has been our purpose to contribute to a clarification and a deeper understanding of the issues and problems that confront us together.

At the same time it must be recognized that the actual situation which Churches in different parts of the world face in their relationships to one another are extremely diverse. Where there are problems in these relationships, they can generally best be dealt with by the Churches themselves within a particular geographical area—local, national or regional—as they confront one another.

Where there are problems in the relationships of Churches to one another, we believe that solutions will be found not so much by rules and regulations as by right attitudes and reconciling actions.

Moreover, even if rules and regulations were desirable, the World Council of Churches by its nature and according to its constitution has neither the authority nor the intent to exercise control over the member Churches or to legislate for them, and is indeed explicitly prevented by its constitution from doing so. It is even more obvious that the World Council cannot control Churches or religious groups which have no relation to it. The influence of its statements derives from their intrinsic merit and from the fact that they express the convictions of responsible representatives of the Churches.

Having due regard for the nature of the ecumenical fellowship represented by the World Council of Churches, we at the same time recognize certain principles which we believe should guide Churches in their mutual relationships and which, if followed, might provide objective and generally applicable standards of practice.

The principles here set forth lay no claim to finality. We have found, however, that they are already receiving sympathetic consideration in many of the member Churches. The following principles are set forth in the hope and belief that they may be helpful to the Churches as they examine their own situation, and that they may provide Churches and councils of Churches with a useful basis for further study and consideration on a local, national and regional basis of the issues treated in this report:

1. That we in our Churches respect the convictions of other Churches whose conception and practice of Church membership differs from our own and consider it our Christian duty to pray for one another and to help each other rise above our respective shortcomings through frank theological interchange, experiences of common worship and concrete acts of mutual service; and that we recognize it as our obligation, when in exceptional cases private or public criticism of another Church seems to be required of us, first to examine ourselves and always to speak the truth in love and to the edification of the Churches;

2. That we recognize it as the primary duty of every awakened Christian to strive prayerfully for the renewal of that Church in which he is a member;

3. That we recognize the right of the mature individual to change his Church allegiance if he becomes convinced that such change of allegiance is God's will for him;

4. That since grave obstacles to brotherly relationships between Churches are created when some Churches are denied the religious liberty which is accorded to others, all Christians should work toward the establishing and maintenance of religious liberty for all Churches and all their members in every land;

5. That we disavow any Church action by which material or social advantages are offered to influence a person's Church affiliation, or undue pressures are brought to bear on persons in times of helplessness or stress;

6. That while it is proper for Churches to make clear their position with regard to marriages between persons belonging to different communions, the conscientious decision of marriage partners as to their future Church allegiance should be respected;

7. That before a young child is received into the membership of a Church other than that of the present affiliation of the parents or guardian, a due pastoral concern for the unity of the family should be exercised; and where the proposed change of affiliation is contrary to the desire of those directly responsible for the child's nurture and upbringing, he (or she) should not be received into the membership of the other Church unless there be reasons of exceptional weight;

8. That due pastoral care should be exercised before receiving anyone into the membership of a Church if he is already, as the member of another Church, under discipline by that Church, or if there is evidence that his reasons for seeking membership in a different Church are worldly or unworthy;

9. That whenever a member of one Church desires to be received into the membership of another Church, direct consultation should be sought between the Churches concerned; but if conscientious motives and sound reasons are apparent, no obstacle should be placed in the way of such change of membership before or after its accomplishment;

10. That while there may be situations where

a Church already present in a given area seems to be so inadequate in its witness to Christ as to call for more faithful witness and proclamation of the Gospel to its members, the first effort of other Churches should be patiently to help that Church toward its renewal and the strengthening of its own witness and ministry;

11. That we should aid Churches in areas where they are already at work, by offering fraternal workers and exchanges of personnel as well as by sharing knowledge and skills and resources, rather than by establishing a competing mission of some other Church.

In our relationships in the World Council of Churches, the member Churches are all called to show such restraint in their exercise of religious liberty as to avoid the causing of offense, and in the fullest possible measure to respect the convictions of other Churches. We therefore call upon the member Churches to disavow proselytism as defined in this report.

We believe that the member Churches should be asked to give thoughtful and prayerful consideration to the matters with which this report is concerned, so that in their dealings with each other they may be mindful of the obligation inherent in the ecumenical fellowship.

The third Assembly at New Delhi, upon receiving this report, issued its own Statement on Religious Liberty.

Statement on Religious Liberty

Mankind is threatened by many forces which curtail or deny freedom. There is accordingly urgent need to reinvigorate efforts to ensure that every person has opportunity for the responsible exercise of religious freedom.

Christians see religious liberty as a consequence of God's creative work, of his redemption of man in Christ and his calling of men into his service. God's redemptive dealing with men is not coercive. Accordingly, human attempts by legal enactment or by pressure of social custom to coerce or to eliminate faith are violations of the fundamental ways of God with men. The freedom which God has given in Christ implies a free response to God's love and the responsibility to serve fellowmen at the point of deepest need.

Holding a distinctive Christian basis for religious liberty, we regard this right as fundamental for men everywhere.

We reaffirm the Declaration on Religious Liberty adopted by the World Council of Churches and the International Missionary Council in August-September, 1948, and hold to its provisions. We recognize the Universal Declaration of Human Rights, proclaimed by the United Nations in December, 1948, as an important instrument in promoting respect for and observance of human rights and fundamental freedoms.

Although freedoms of every kind are interrelated, religious liberty may be considered as a distinctive human right, which all men may exercise no matter what their faith. The article on religious freedom in the Universal Declaration is an acceptable standard, always provided that it be given a comprehensive interpretation.

Everyone has the right to freedom of thought, conscience and religion; this right includes freedom to change his religion or belief, and freedom, either alone or in community with others and in public or private, to manifest his religion or belief in teaching, practice, worship and observance.

The recognition of the inherent dignity and of the equal and inalienable rights of all members of the human family requires that the general standard here declared should be given explicit expression in every aspect of society. Without seeking to be inclusive, we illustrate as follows:

Freedom to manifest one's religion or belief, in public or in private and alone or in community with others, is essential to the expression of inner freedom.

It includes freedom to worship according to one's chosen form, in public or in private.

It includes freedom to teach, whether by formal or informal instruction, as well as preaching with a view to propagating one's faith and persuading others to accept it.

It includes freedom to practice religion or belief, whether by performance of acts of mercy or by the expression in word or deed of the implications of belief in social, economic and political matters, both domestic and international.

It includes freedom of observance by following religious customs or by participating in religious rites in the family or in public meeting.

*Religious liberty includes freedom to change
one's religion or belief without consequent social,
economic and political disabilities. Implicit in this
right is the right freely to maintain one's belief
or disbelief without external coercion or dis-
ability.*

*The exercise of religious liberty involves other
human rights.* The Universal Declaration proclaims, among others, the right to freedom of
peaceful assembly and association; the right to freedom of opinion and expression, including freedom to seek, receive and impart information and
ideas through any media and regardless of fron-
tiers; the prior right of parents to choose the kind
of education that shall be given to their children;
freedom to participate in choosing the desired
form of government and in freely electing officials;
freedom from the retroactive application of penal
law; and freedom to leave and to return to one's
country, and to seek asylum elsewhere.

*The freedom with which Christ has set us
free calls forth responsibility for the rights of
others. The civil freedom which we claim in the
name of Christ must be freely available for all
men to exercise responsibly. It is the corresponding obligation of governments and of society
to ensure the exercise of these civil rights without
discrimination. It is for the Churches in their own
life and witness, recognizing their own past failures
in this regard, to play their indispensable role in
promoting the realization of religious liberty for
all men.*

During the four sessions of Vatican Council II,
the WCC watched carefully—and realistically—the
development of *De libertate religiosa.* The WCC ob-

servers to the council, as well as those delegated directly by the Churches, contributed suggestions to the Unity Secretariat as it did the successive drafting.

Soon after the promulgation of the final text, the Central Committee, in February 1966, stated:

"We welcome with satisfaction the Vatican Council's *Declaration on Religious Freedom* with its clear statements proclaiming full civil religious freedom, both individual and collective, for everybody, everywhere. . . . We are encouraged by the fact that there is now a large measure of agreement among all the Churches in these matters. . . . We hope that, on the basis of their statements of religious liberty, from now on all the Churches will be able to take a common stand for the full application of the principle of religious liberty in all parts of the world and in all possible action to ensure the observance of this principle."

The WCC Secretariat on Religious Liberty has made a careful study (unpublished), in parallel columns, of the Vatican Council Declaration and the Statements made at Amsterdam in 1948 and at New Delhi in 1961. The study shows fundamental agreement in eight areas: (1) the general principle of the right to freedom in religious matters, and the universality of this right; (2) individual religious freedom; (3) religious freedom of the family (Vatican Council II emphasizes parents' religious guidance and "true freedom" in choice of schools, whereas the WCC stresses "sources of information" and the "religious point of view to which their children shall be exposed");

(4) freedom of religious assembly and association; (5) corporate religious freedom (open and public worship, teaching, ministry, property-holding, international communication); (6) the universal duty (binding on Churches and believers, civil authorities and citizens) to uphold these rights; (7) the nature of civil authority (whose paramount duty is to protect human rights); (8) moderating norms.

The First Report of the Joint Working Group between the Roman Catholic Church and the World Council of Churches (Feb. 1966) listed "the practical consequences of religious liberty and problems presented by proselytism" as a major issue for further study. This Report was approved by the WCC Central Commission and the authorities of the Holy See. In May, 1966, the working group decided to set up a commission to deal with "the question of proselytism in the light of the Church's obligation to witness, of the principles of religious freedom, and of the common ecumenical task".

In conclusion: The passing of the Declaration as an *act of the Church* presents a far more demanding ecumenical challenge. Rather than waste energy on charges and countercharges *within* the Christian family, the Christian Churches can co-operate in building into the convictions and conduct of hundreds of millions of Christians the content of religious freedom statements, in proclaiming before the secular powers the religious rights of all men everywhere, and in reflecting together on the more basic Christian question: What is this freedom *for?*

Part Two

Religious Freedom and the World Council of Churches*

by

Dr. Lukas Vischer

When we compare the *Declaration on Religious Freedom* of Vatican Council II with the texts produced by the general assemblies of the World Council of Churches in Amsterdam (1948) and New Delhi (1961), we see at once that there is a large measure of agreement. Furthermore, if we disregard the theological reasoning on which they are based, we see that, insofar as the principle itself and its practical application are concerned, the texts are often almost identical. This similarity is not accidental, and its importance can hardly be overrated, for it points up a convergence of the Churches in facing certain common questions that arise from the constantly changing conditions of modern society.

It is true that the Churches start from different premises. But in their attempt to understand the task of the Church in the modern world they repeatedly achieve common insights on the basis of that common foundation which unites them in spite of all differences. The various declarations on religious freedom are a particularly clear illustration of this. The different premises from which the individual Churches proceed become evident in the diverse arguments advanced in behalf of reli-

* This article, printed here in its entirety, appeared in *Concilium* 18: *Religious Freedom* (Glen Rock, New Jersey: Paulist Press [1966]), pp. 53-63.

gious freedom. The World Council shows that no exhaustive argument is possible. Nonetheless, the decisive statement that every individual has the right to confess his religious conviction publicly and that this right must be protected is shared in common by the Churches.

Does this admission create additional responsibility? Shouldn't it be formulated and developed? Is it enough simply to state the fact that agreement exists; shouldn't we rather try to draw the logical consequences? The Churches would not be taking their commitment to ecumenism seriously enough if they did not decide to pursue these issues together.

I

THREE FIELDS OF APPLICATION

If we want to understand in what sense the documents of the World Council use the term "religious freedom", we have to distinguish three different fields in which it is applied. The discussion of religious freedom currently in progress within the ecumenical movement was originally involved with the question of *Church and State*. The Church must be free from all State control and protection, and even when the Church is not left the necessary freedom to preach the Gospel, it must nevertheless always see to it that the State does not overstep its permissible limits. The discussion then passed directly to religious freedom as a *principle of order within the State*, particularly as a *condition for the life of an international society*. It is from this aspect that the Declarations of Amsterdam and New Delhi develop the question. The more progress the ecumenical movement

made and the more deeply the separated Churches
became aware of what they had in common, the
more urgent the question of religious freedom became in the *relations of the Churches among themselves*. The report on "Christian Witness, Religious Freedom and Proselytism", accepted at New
Delhi, examined the issue in this light and showed
to what extent respect for the principle of religious
freedom is the unconditional presupposition for
any communion and intercourse between the separated Churches.

These three fields of application are of course
closely connected, and it is impossible to deal with
one without indirectly touching upon the other
two. Yet they must be distinguished, particularly
when we wish to relate the Declaration of Vatican
Council II with those of the World Council. *Vatican Council II's Declaration only deals with religious freedom in the second of these three ways,*
and while it touches upon the question of Church
and State, it does not treat the problem explicitly.
The role that religious freedom plays in deepening the ecumenical relationship is not mentioned
at all. However much agreement there may be,
therefore, we must realize from the start that the
scope of the problem is not yet identical for all
parties concerned.

II

POINTS TO BE DEVELOPED

Let us briefly survey the earliest beginnings of
of the discussion within the ecumenical context
and select the most important points that have
already contributed to the development of our
theme.

1. *The Relationship between Church and State*

The inauguration of the ecumenical movement coincided with a much wider upheaval in the traditional relationship between Church and State in the West, particularly within the countries of Europe. While at the beginning of this century one could still cherish the idea that Church and State form a unity and that the Church was in a certain sense the soul of the State and was therefore entitled to certain privileges corresponding to the services it might render, this position became decidedly less tenable after World War I. The political upheavals and revolutions that marked the postwar years; the rapid increase and growing influence of movements, parties and groups that rejected any connection with the Church or were even hostile to it; the more extensive mixing of the population, even in regions where up till then one denomination had predominated; the growing importance of new nations that were anxious to assert their own religion and culture—all these factors shook the more or less conscious assumption that a given Church could take for granted that the inhabitants of a given region were its members. This was certainly not something new. The close ties which formerly bound Church and State together were already broken in the 18th and, especially, the 19th centuries. But the first decades of this century did bring about a decided acceleration of the process, and the Churches were no longer able to ignore the fact that they were a minority within their own nation. This was a particularly severe realization for the great Protestant Churches of Europe, for due to historical circumstances they had assumed especially close ties with the State and had practically no supranational bond with one another.

The great ecumenical Oxford Conference (1937) mentioned this fact mainly as a challenge to the Churches: "The Church has not yet faced the new situation with sufficient frankness. With the conservative instincts of all institutions of long standing and influence it has fought a defensive—and on the whole a losing—battle for the maintenance of as much as possible of the old ideal of *Corpus Christianum* and of the privileges and authorities which that implies. . . . The Church finds itself today in a new relation to the community. . . . Domination it cannot have and possibly ought not to desire. . . . It is challenged to find a new understanding of its duty to the common life."[1]

2. *The Missions and the New Churches*

This new understanding was not imposed on the Churches solely from without. It also grew from within the life of the Churches themselves. The missionary movement, and above all the gradual emergence of "young Churches", prepared the way for a new and deeper understanding of the nature of the Church. Missionary experience demonstrated that the Church must be understood as a special community called by God for the purpose of proclaiming the message of God's kingdom. The question concerning the nature of the Church in relation to all worldly and human institutions profoundly stirred theological thought during the years subsequent to World War I. It was becoming increasingly clear that through its close links with nation and State the Church had obscured its own nature and mission; as a consequence its claim to authenticity had to suffer. We only have to recall the sharp attacks launched by the Swiss theologian Karl Barth against identifying the Church with

---

[1] *The Churches Survey Their Task* (Oxford, 1937), pp. 200-1.

anything that might be labeled "Christian". The authentic meaning of freedom was at the very center of this debate. The Word of God as the sole absolute over against man bestows a freedom such as no human source can provide and as no human society—unfortunately not even the Church, at times —can realize. It becomes real only in the degree to which provision is made for that Word of God.

The debate might not have had such important consequences for the ecumenical movement if it had not assumed practical significance during the rule of Nazism in Germany. The Church suddenly came face to face with a State founded upon an ideology wholly opposed to it. The only way it could proclaim its message was first to liberate itself from the bonds which tied it to the State. The foundation of the "confessing Church" was an attempt to preserve the Church's freedom within a Church and a State that were menaced by a false ideology or had already yielded to it.

What happened in Germany was not without its consequences for the other Churches. They had to decide where and how they could recognize the true Church. The questions evoked by the Church's struggle in Germany were equally valid for Churches in other countries, and consequently it is not at all astonishing that the Oxford Conference of 1937 dealt in detail with the nature of those freedoms the Church could claim from the State. A tentative list of these freedoms was drafted: freedom of religious doctrine, preaching and education, freedom to determine the organization of the Church, freedom to do missionary work and to cooperate with the Churches of other countries and freedom to enjoy the same rights as other groups in the same State, such as the right to property, etc.[2]

---

[2] *Ibid.*, pp. 84-5.

The discussion necessarily expanded: the Churches could hardly claim freedom for themselves without likewise claiming it for others. Following the "golden rule", the freedom it claimed for itself would have to be applicable to all. This conclusion was already explicitly accepted by the Oxford Conference: "In pleading for such rights we do not ask for any privilege to be granted to Christians that is denied to others. While the liberty with which Christ has set us free can neither be given nor destroyed by any government, Christians because of that inner freedom are both jealous for its outward expression and solicitous that all men should have freedom in religious life. The rights which Christian discipleship demands are such as are good for all men, and no nation has ever suffered by reason of granting such liberties." [3]

3. *International Organization*

These considerations acquired additional urgency due to the question regarding the foundations on which an international society could be created and maintained, and insofar as modern technological and ecumenical developments linked individual States more closely together, the need for an answer became more pressing. The founding of the United Nations underlined this need. The non-Roman Catholic Churches found themselves in a difficult position. Since practically all of them were closely associated with some form of nationalism, they could hardly find the principles to solve the problem within the inventory of their own resources. It is therefore not astonishing that the ecumenical movement became preoccupied with the problem. From the very outset religious freedom

---

[3] *Ibid.*, pp. 184-5.

was considered an essential condition for a viable international organization. The Oxford Conference did not really deal with this in a creative fashion, but all the same it emphatically declared that religious freedom was one of the basic principles: "Freedom of religion is an essential element in a better international order. This is an implication of the faith of the Church. Moreover, the ecumenical character of the Church compels it to view the question of religious freedom as an international problem. . . ." [4] The text briefly explained what was meant by this principle and emphasized that Christians cannot exploit the power of their nation to secure unjust privileges within another nation—a statement that was anything but obvious at that time.

But it was not until World War II and the years which followed it that the theme was seriously tackled. During the war (as far as circumstances allowed) the Research Secretariat of the World Council for Practical Christianity made a study on international organization, and the various exchanges in this connection showed increasing agreement on the point that freedom of the individual's conscience guaranteed by the State was a basic principle for the creation of an international community. William Temple, Archbishop of York and later Archbishop of Canterbury, made a remarkable contribution to the discussion.

After the war, the thread was picked up with renewed determination. But in the meantime the context of the discussion had changed. The United Nations had actually been founded, and the *Declaration on the Basic Rights of Man* was receiving public attention. It is against this background that we must see the declarations of the

---

[4] *Ibid.*, p. 184.

World Council at Amsterdam (1948) and New
Delhi (1961). They maintain that every man has the
right to religious freedom because of his God-given
dignity and that this right must be guaranteed to
every individual as well as to every religion and
religious group. These declarations specify in detail
those rights which involve religious freedom and
which the Churches must allow to prevail both for
themselves and for others. Of all the statements
made by the World Council, these two declarations
come closest to that of Vatican Council II. Both
the general substance and many individual statements are almost identical. In any case, the conciliar
Declaration is partly motivated by this same preoccupation with international order. Among the
differences between them, I may point out that the
World Council explicitly bases the principle of
religious freedom on non-religious convictions.[5]

In comparing the conciliar Declaration with
those of the World Council, we should not forget
that the latter do not bind the individual Churches
in the same way a conciliar decree binds the Roman
Catholic Church. Furthermore, although the consensus has been reached and no Church has objected
to the statement, not all the Churches have as yet
pursued all its consequences. The Department for
Religious Freedom and the Commission of the
Churches for International Affairs are the two
agencies of the World Council charged with studying the problems implied in the affirmation of religious freedom and the practical steps to be taken
to translate it into reality.

4. *Contact between the Separated Churches*

One final aspect must be mentioned which has
moved the issue of religious freedom into the fore-

[5] For a detailed comparison, cf. A. F. Carrillo de Albornoz
in *Ecumenical Review* 1 (1966).

ground of the ecumenical movement: the encounter of the separated Churches themselves. For the non-Roman Churches the ecumenical movement was not inaugurated merely to precipitate dialogue. They felt from the start the need to work together as a community. This was particularly acute on the international level, for if the Churches were to bear witness in the international arena, they would have to do so in common. But how could Churches with different and often even contradictory convictions, with different historical backgrounds and different national and cultural characters form a single community? If this was ever to come about, the recognition of the principle of religious liberty would have to be the first and unconditional presupposition. The community could only grow on the common recognition of each other's freedom. The Oxford Conference was clear on this point, although quite evidently it did not pursue the problem and all its ramifications: "We call upon the Churches we represent to guard against the sin of themselves conniving at repression of Churches and religious bodies of a faith and order differing from their own." [6] The report goes even further. It regards this mutual respect as an opportunity for Christian witness, since it is by setting an example of mutual tolerance that the Churches actually promote international understanding.

However, it goes without saying that a community of Churches cannot be built on the principle of religious freedom alone. The bonds which link the Churches in the name of Christ are too strong to find adequate expression in the mere recognition of this principle. Yet just such a recognition is certainly a preliminary condition if that deeper communion in Christ is to become visible.

---

[6] *The Churches Survey Their Task, op. cit.*, p. 185.

Only if the Churches recognize each other's freedom to bear witness can they really meet, grow together and eventually bear witness in common. As their communion deepens and expands, the Churches will observe rules in their intercourse which go beyond the mere principle of religious freedom.

The right to religious freedom is a civil right. When the Churches speak of religious freedom, they speak of rights that are incorporated in civil law and protected by the State for all its citizens. Moreover, although the Churches must respect these rights, they cannot simply confine their efforts to standing by and respecting each other's witness. Their communion in Christ imposes upon them a positive responsibility for each other, and it will lead them farther into a mutual relationship which is beyond that which the law can enforce. This is particularly clear in the problem of proselytism. A Church which tries to attract the members of another Church by non-spiritual means makes it impossible for the Churches to live together; therefore, the practice must be excluded. But actually only the coarsest forms of proselytism are an offense against religious freedom as a civil right; the more subtle forms can only be eliminated when the Churches become aware through the spiritual foundations of their community that they are responsible for each other and contribute to their mutual sanctification.

The World Council had to face this problem in all its acuteness. The Churches had founded a community, and each member was aware that he had bound himself to the truth. They were determined to work with each other. What was the result? The Report on "Christian Witness, Religious Freedom and Proselytism within the Framework of the World Council of Churches" (New

Delhi, 1961) gave a preliminary accounting. It not only showed what religious freedom would mean for mutual relations between the Churches, but it also stated some demands which were only to be understood as involving an "ecumenical obligation".

Vatican Council II barely treated this aspect of religious freedom. The *Constitution on the Church* and, above all, the *Decree on Ecumenism* and the *Pastoral Constitution on the Church in the Modern World* provided some clues that may lead to a broadening of the issue. An ecumenical discussion is desirable; not only would it clarify the position for both sides, but it could also have numerous practical consequences.

If the discussion is going to be pursued, one question in particular must be treated in depth, a question which has found no answer in the documents of either the World Council or Vatican Council II: How far is the Church itself a community based on freedom? The Church is held together by the common confession of the Gospel. How much difference does this confession allow? Where must we draw the line between a plurality that strengthens the witness to Christ and a plurality that destroys it? Most texts dealing with religious freedom neglect to speak of the freedom that must prevail within the Church. But if the community is to grow and especially if the Churches themselves are expected to set "an example of freedom to all"—as the Oxford Conference put it—then this question is of decisive importance. It cannot be regarded as a purely private matter and be withheld from the ecumenical dialogue; on the contrary, precisely from the point of view of witness it must be included.

III
CONCLUSION

Once again we are back to the suggestion we made at the outset, namely that the Churches should formulate their convictions about religious freedom in common and should arrive at an explicit and common declaration of these convictions. While this would certainly provide a broader basis for the mutual relationship between the Churches, it is not the ultimate reason. Such a community could in itself be a witness in a world which is crying out for a more stable order. By renouncing in common every kind of domination, the Churches would be in a position to witness against any power that might claim to be absolute. By their awareness of a common bond and a common service in Christ they would be able to show forth the meaning of this bond in truth. There is no need to stress the value of such a witness in a world whose order is imperiled by a false absolutism on the one hand and is undermined by indifference toward the truth as the source of life on the other.

Selected Bibliography

I

ON THE DECLARATION ITSELF

Bea, Augustin Cardinal, "Religious Freedom." *The Catholic Mind,* LXII, (May, 1964), pp. 4-16.
——— "The Church and Religious Freedom." *The Month,* XXXV, No. 5, (May, 1966), pp. 267-277.
Carillo de Albornoz, A. F., "Religious Liberty and the Second Vatican Council." *The Ecumenical Review,* XVI, No. 4, (July, 1964), pp. 395-405.
——— "Religious Freedom: Intrinsic or Fortuitous?" *The Christian Century,* LXXXII, (Sept. 15, 1965), pp. 1122-1126.
——— "The Ecumenical and World Significance of the Vatican Declaration on Religious Liberty." *The Ecumenical Review,* XVIII, No. 1, (Jan. 1966), pp. 1-27.
Daniélou, Jean, S.J., "Religious Liberty." *Journal of Ecumenical Studies,* II, No. 2, (Spring, 1965), pp. 265-271.
Herder Correspondence, unsigned articles on the successive drafts and conciliar debates, I, No. 7, (July, 1964), pp. 202-208; 12, (Dec., 1964), pp. 352-355; II, No. 8, (August, 1965), p. 271; III, No. 3, (March, 1966), pp. 79-85.
Kelly, Dean M. and Nelson, Claud D., "Religious Liberty: Toward Consensus." *The Christian Century,* LXXXIII, (May 18, 1966), pp. 651-653.

Littell, Franklin H., "A Response to the Declaration." *The Documents of Vatican II,* Walter M. Abbott, S.J., ed. New York: Guild, America and Association Presses, 1966, pp. 697-700.

Love, Thomas T., "De Libertate Religiosa: An Interpretative Analysis." *A Journal of Church and State,* II, (Winter, 1966).

Murray, John Courtney, S.J., "On Religious Liberty." *America,* CIX, (Nov. 30, 1965), pp. 704-706.

——— "The Problem of Religious Freedom." *Theological Studies,* XXV, (Dec., 1964), pp. 503-575; this appeared under the same title in book form by Newman Press, 1965.

——— "This Matter of Religious Freedom." *America,* CXII, (Jan. 9, 1965), pp. 40-43.

——— "The Declaration on Religious Freedom: Its Deeper Significance." *America,* CXIV, (April 23, 1966), pp. 592-593.

——— "Commentary." *The Documents of Vatican II,* Walter M. Abbott, S.J., ed. New York: Guild, America and Association Presses, 1966, pp. 672-674; also cf. his thorough footnoting to the Declaration, pp. 675-696.

——— "The Declaration on Religious Freedom." *Vatican II: An Inter-Faith Appraisal.* New York: Association Press, 1966.

Religious Liberty: An End and a Beginning, J. C. Murray, S.J., ed. New York: Macmillan, 1966.

II
Background Reading

Bévenot, Maurice, S.J., "Thesis and Hypothesis." *Theological Studies,* XV, No. 3, (Sept., 1954), pp. 440-446.

Blau, Joseph, ed., *Cornerstones of Religious Freedom in America*. New York, Harper Torchbook.

Boyer, Charles, S.J., "Truth and Tolerance." *Unitas* (Eng. ed.), XV, No. 2, (Spring, 1962), pp. 3-16.

Carillo de Albornoz, A. F., *Roman Catholicism and Religious Liberty*. Geneva: World Council of Churches, 1959.

――― *The Basis of Religious Liberty*. New York: Association Press, 1963.

――― *Religious Liberty in the World: A General Review of the World Situation in 1965*. Geneva: World Council of Churches, 1966.

Christian and Religious Liberty: essays by John C. Bennett, William Ball, Paul Kauper, John B. Sheerin. *The Catholic World*, (September, 1965).

D'Arcy, Eric, *Conscience and Its Right to Freedom*. London: Sheed and Ward, 1961.

Ehler, Sidney Z., *Twenty Centuries of Church and State*. Westminster: Newman Press, 1957.

Hartmann, Albert, S.J., "Religionsfreiheit in Catholic Theology." *The Ecumenical Review*, XIII, No. 3, (July, 1961), pp. 427-433.

Hurley, Denis E., "The Church-State Dilemma." *The Furrow*, (March, 1963), pp. 141-147.

Lercaro, Giacomo Cardinal, "Religious Tolerance and Catholic Tradition." *The Catholic Mind*, LVIII, No. 2, (Feb., 1960), pp. 12-24.

Lecler, Joseph, S.J., *Tolerance and the Reformation*, trans. by T. L. Westow, 2 vols. New York: Association Press, 1960.

McDonagh, Edna, "Tolerance: An Appreciation of the Person." *The Furrow*, XII, No. 1, (Jan., 1961), pp. 49-55.

Main Ecumenical Statements on Principles concerning Religious Freedom. Geneva: World Council of Churches, 1965.

Miller, Perry, *Roger Williams: His Contribution to the American Tradition*. Peter Smith, 1953.

Murray, John Courtney, S.J., "Religious Freedom." *Freedom and Man*, J. C. Murray, ed. New York: Kenedy, 1965, pp. 131-140.

——— *We Hold These Truths: Catholic Reflections on the American Proposition*. New York: Sheed and Ward, 1960.

Newman, Jeremiah, "Charity and Tolerance." *Irish Ecclesiastical Record*, IX, No. 4, (April, 1961), pp. 236-247.

Niebuhr, H. Richard, *The Kingdom of God in America*. Harper Torchbook, 1959.

Religious Freedom in America: essays by John Tracy Ellis, Franklin H. Littell, Bertram W. Korn, Edward Duff, Sidney Hook reprinted from *Cross Currents,* (Winter, 1963), pub. by National Conference of Christians and Jews.

Smith, Elwyn, ed., *Church-State Relations in Ecumenical Perspective*. Pittsburgh: Duquesne University Press, 1966.

St. John, Henry, O.P., "Tolerance and Conscience." *Blackfriars,* XIII, (July-Aug., 1961), pp. 288-297.

Tolerance and the Catholic, a series of essays. Trans. by George Lamb. New York: Sheed and Ward, 1955.

Wright, John J., "Freedom and Conscience." *The Critic,* (April-May, 1964), pp. 11-28.

APR 11 '97